1-31-01

Crazy Quilt

A Patchwork of New and Collected Poems

Life is Good!!
Elizabeth Ebert

Crazy Quilt

A Patchwork of New and Collected Poems

Elizabeth Ebert

Thunder Hawk Press
Lemmon, South Dakota

Cover design by Michael Dougherty, Type & Graphics, Bozeman, MT

Library of Congress Catalog Data
Main entry under Western poetry

ISBN	Soft Cover	0-9657082-0-9
	Hard Cover	0-9657082-1-7

Other books by Elizabeth Ebert:

*Grand River Tales and Other Poems**
*Trails to Thunder Hawk**
*The Pickup Cowgirl**

*Included in this book

Published by:

Thunder Hawk Press

Elizabeth Ebert
10930 208th Ave
Lemmon SD 57638

Dedicated with love
to
my husband, S. J.,
who has shared the last
half-century of my life,

and to our children,
Jonni, John and Jayne

FOREWORD

I have always written poetry, but I did it secretly, periodically consigning my efforts to the fire. Then, in 1989, a bit irritated by a chance remark that my husband had made, I found the courage to stand up at the Badlands Cowboy Poetry Gathering in Medora, North Dakota, and recite some of my verses. It opened up a whole new world for me. I treasure the memories of the places it has taken me and the people I have met these past few years.. I have enjoyed the fellowship and camaraderie of these western poets, and I especially wish to thank Baxter Black for smoothing my way, Gwen Peterson for her friendship and expertise, and Mike Logan for his encouragement. Life is good!

--Elizabeth Ebert

TABLE OF CONTENTS

TABLE OF CONTENTS, CONTINUED

TABLE OF CONTENTS, CONTINUED

I was born on the prairie and somehow I cannot envision living anywhere else

I KNOW ABOUT THE PRAIRIE

I know about the prairie
Where the wind blows fresh and free,
Where grasses sway and shimmer,
Undulating like the sea.

I do not know the desert
With mesquite and prickly pear,
And its air of silent mystery
I am an alien there.

But I know rocky hilltops
And meadowlarks that sing,
And valleys with their little creeks
That only run in spring.

I do not know the mountains
With peaks that touch the sky
With rivers wild and canyons dark
Where none could hear my cry.

But I know prairie sunshine
And open fields to roam,
And if home is where the heart is,
Then the prairie is my home.

ut

Back in the days when I was young and impressionable- - ! !

I USED TO LOVE COWBOYS

I once loved cowboys in my youth
This is the plain unvarnished truth.
Young men in chaps and snug-fit pants
Who rode with studied nonchalance,
Adept with lariat and quirt.
Their sunburned cheeks, eyes made to flirt,
And curls beneath a cowboy hat
Could make my heart go pit-a-pat.

But through the years, I've changed somehow.
I view with mild amusement now
Those slim young men in cowboy boots
Who lounge against the bucking chutes
And talk of only ride and rope.
I like someone of broader scope,
Someone with visions in his eyes
That sees beyond a buckle prize.
Whose life is more than rodeo
Who likes to plan and build and grow,

Who cares for poetry and books.
I'm less concerned about his looks;
I'll tolerate a little fat,
Some baldness 'neath that cowman's hat----

That COWMAN'S hat? Upon my word,
I haven't changed -- I've just matured!

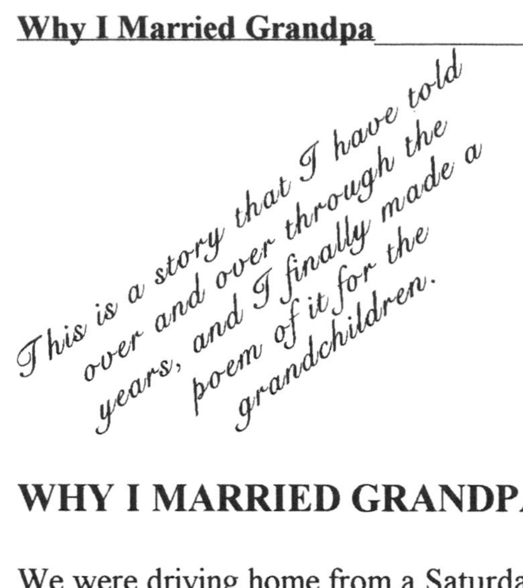

WHY I MARRIED GRANDPA

We were driving home from a Saturday date,
Just a local dance and it wasn't late,
So, when we got within a mile
We decided to park for a little while.
Now the coupe he was driving was shiny black,
He'd bought it as soon as he got back
From Italy when the war was through,
Just a straight-stick Ford and it wasn't new,
But 'twas warm in that Southwind heater's glow,
And with '40s tunes on the radio
We could almost forget the cold outside-----
At least we could, 'til the motor died.

He tried the starter but it was no use,
The battery was drained of all its juice.
Now a man from this modern generation
Would have thrown up his hands in desperation.
For 'twas wintertime as you've been told
And the snow was deep and the night was cold.
But he said, "Now don't you get upset,

I'll get this Ford restarted yet!"
So from one hind tire he scooped the snow,
Jacked up that wheel as high as 'twould go,
Turned on the switch, put the car in gear,
And he spun that wheel there in the rear
With a two-handed spin, while I stood and gazed,
Completely and thoroughly amazed.

And in less time than you'd ever thought
That engine fired and then it caught,
And somehow, mixed with that motor's sound
A thought came to me, so profound.
And I said to myself, "Hey, listen, kid,
That's the man to marry." So I did!
And down through the years when life got rough
And times were hard and things were tough,
It sure was a comfort to me, knowing
He'd spin some wheels and get things going.

By the way,
we still drive Fords!

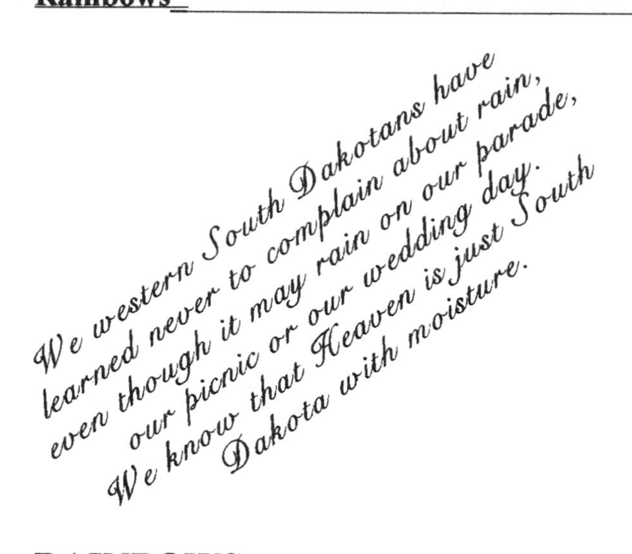

RAINBOWS

The rain came down in torrents, endlessly,
 For forty days and nights the skies were dark,
And long and fervent were the prayers raised up
 By Noah and his people in the Ark.

Their prayers were answered with a rainbow bright,
 A covenant, a promise in the sky.
And Noah and his people disembarked
 With gratitude upon an earth grown dry.

Another year of drouth has parched our land,
 The dust clouds blow across the barren plain,
And now we pray a different sort of prayer:
 "Oh, Lord, don't send us rainbows--
 send us RAIN!"

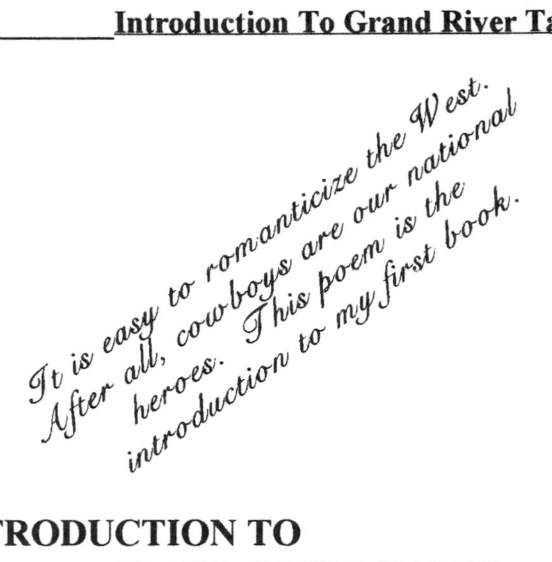

INTRODUCTION TO GRAND RIVER TALES

You've heard of the West of story and rhyme,
Of golden folk from a golden time
When the range was young and life was free
And a man could be what a man should be.
When a horse and a saddle were all you'd need,
And every deed was a golden deed.
When the ranchers only fought to keep
Their rightful range from the dad-blamed sheep
And even the rustlers lived with dash.
And died for their deeds with a grand panache.

And the women! The very word was sweet!
The men all clustered about their feet
For they were gentle and good and wise
With long, long hair and laughing eyes.
The dance hall girls, though brassy and bold,
Always had a heart of gold,

For they searched through the west for an outlaw
brother
To take him home to a dying mother.
And the Madames were all like Matt's Miss Kitty,
And the schoolmarm's, they were so doggone pretty,
And naturally they all were smart,
They won the kids' and the cowboys' heart.
And the ranchers' wives, through wind and weather,
Kept their man and the ranch together.
This is the West of story and rhyme.
Of golden folk from a golden time.

Now let's look at the West as it really was.
But only a moment's glance because
When we shine a light on the past's dim mirror
To make the images stand out clearer,
We see the greed and the hate and the hurt,
And the sorrow and shame and the death and the
dirt.
And as we study their imperfection,
We see too much of our own reflection.

The poem that follows is the first of the Grand River Tales.

THE SWAMPER FROM TRAIL'S END BAR

Ed was trailin' cows with a Texas crew,
He must have been about twenty-two,
A darned good hand, he was lean and long,
Tougher than rawhide and twice as strong.
A cheerful cuss with a ready laugh,
He sat his horse like a second half.
His hair was curly and his eyes were brown,
And he turned some heads when he came to town.
At least he did. Until the day
He dropped his loop on a proddy stray
And the steer turned back with a lusty bawl,
And the three went over the canyon wall
And rolled to the bottom, mashed and mangled,
With their blood and their bones and their fate
entangled.
Well, the steer was dead, and they shot the horse,
And they dragged Ed out of the watercourse,
And they weren't too sure that he'd last that far
But they packed him in to the Trail's End Bar.
And the boys got together and they took up a purse
And they left him there, for better or worse.
And I guess you could say 'twas a little of each,
'Cause he didn't die, but he lost his speech;
He could get around but he'd never ride
For his leg was all twisted out to the side.

When the bartender saw he was getting better
He said, "Now, Ed, we should write a letter
So your folks could come and take you where
You'd be at home with the proper care."

Ed shuffled up a little nearer
And peered at himself in the back bar mirror.
The battered mouth and the broken nose,
The staring eye that he couldn't close,
The palsied hand and the shrunken frame,
The twisted leg, forever lame,
Then he turned away and he shook his head.
With sudden compassion the bartender said,
"There's fires to fix and there's floors to sweep,
If you want to stay here you can earn your keep."
Ed took a long look about the room
Then he silently nodded and picked up the broom.

So Ed was a fixture from that day,
And he lived in a sad subhuman way,
'Twas not that they meant to be unkind
But you'll have to admit 'twould be hard to find
A common basis to talk and joke
With a man who neither smiled nor spoke,
So they'd buy him a drink and they'd pray to God
They never need travel the road he trod.
Then they'd turn their gaze to the opposite wall
And pretend that he wasn't there at all.

But there was nothing else to do
So Ed stayed on. His wants were few.
His mangled mouth couldn't manage meat
So about the only things he'd eat
Were the hard-boiled eggs that he cooked in a pot
On the stove in back by his narrow cot.
His clothes were what nobody else could use,
And he sewed himself some sheepskin shoes

And he'd shuffle around at his menial chores,
He'd fix the fires and sweep the floors,
And clean spittoons of their crusted spit,
And nobody cared that he drank a bit.
And nobody came who recognized Ed,
And if he knew them, he never said.

And when he'd been there ten years or more,
He stood one night by the barroom door
Staring out at the starry sky,
Then he turned around with a wistful sigh
And he picked up some glasses and drained the
dregs.
Then he took a couple of hard-boiled eggs
Along with a little chunk of bread,
And crumpled down on his narrow bed
To wait 'til the Trail's End closed its doors
And he could get to his swampin' chores.
When the poker game was finally through,
Somewhere along about half-past-two,
The bartender glanced at the tattered heap
And said to himself, "Let the poor wretch sleep!"

But when he returned again, next day,
There in the same place, Ed still lay,
The pulse long gone from his bony wrist,
But the eggs still clutched in his grimy fist.
Well, nobody came the corpse to claim,
No one remembered Ed's last name.
But it's ashes to ashes and dust to dust,
When it comes to buryin', somebody must.
So they got some boards of rough-sawed pine,
Fetched an old blanket the box to line,

The Swamper From Trail's End Bar

But, somehow, none of those men could stand
To pry those eggs from that lifeless hand.
So they hammered the lid over egg and all
And onto the box let the hard clods fall.

There'll be no marble slab at the head
Of a derelict only known as Ed.
But let's pray that God leaves the gate ajar
And welcomes the Swamper from Trail's End Bar.

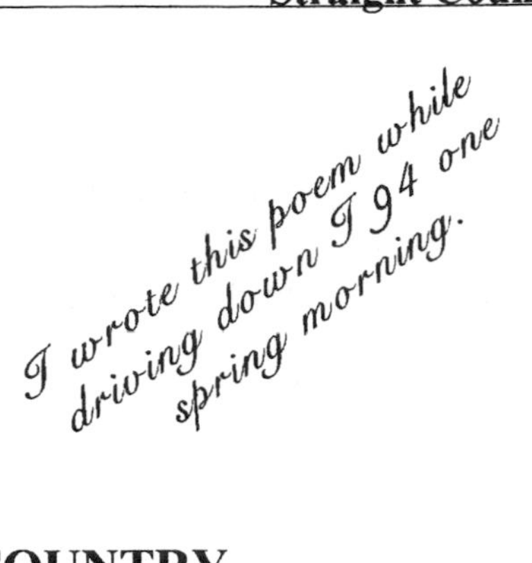

STRAIGHT COUNTRY

Out on the highway the big trucks whine
Eating the miles in a string-straight line
Bordered by fences, marching there
To keep each section to proper square,
Where the tractors roar with an urgent need
To plant straight furrows with springtime seed.
And even the trees in a straight line grow,
Edging each farmstead with sentinel row.

Where the wheels of progress turn with speed,
Straight's a necessity indeed.
But I long for the old days, and wish that I
Had lived when the earth nestled into the sky,
When the buffalo grazed in the belly-deep grass
And the only sounds were the winds as they'd pass.

YOU MAKE ME SO DARNED MAD

You make me so darned mad
I think I'll dye---
My hair. Lose thirty pounds
And then I think that I
Will build a brand new life.
I do not need to be some cowman's wife.

You make me so DARNED mad
This time I swear
I will lose thirty pounds
And dye my hair.
And when I am no longer gray and fat
Why, then I'll leave you flat.

You make me SO DARNED MAD!
---I wonder why
I'm laughing with you now
And baking pie!

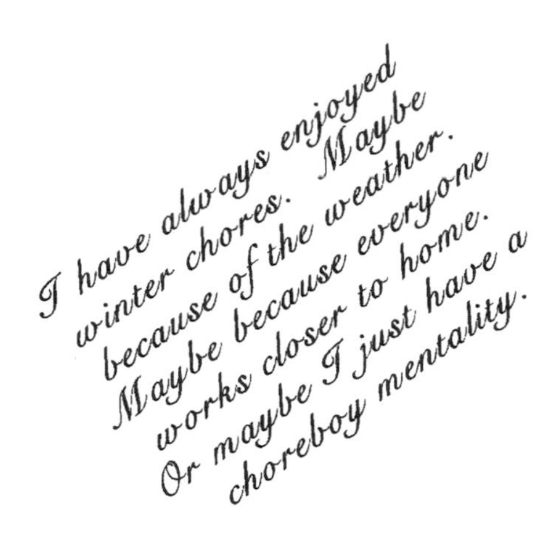

CAKING FIRST-CALF HEIFERS

The morning's crisp and clear and cold.
    The first-calf heifers wait beside the gate.
They jockey for position in the lead,
    And bawl their irritation if I'm late.

I've loudly said, "Young cows need exercise."
    So I've been somehow volunteered to take
Them on their daily constitutional,
    Bribed on their way by promises of cake.

Now bundled snug in winter coveralls,
    In mittens, boots and heavy woolen socks,
I shovel buckets full of cattle cubes,
    Then hoist them up into the pickup box,

And four-wheel off to break a new day's trail
Out to the feeding circle there beyond.
I was a first-child mother once myself
And so perhaps we feel some kindred bond.

And, like a gentle midwife, I explain
The reason why we make this daily trip.
I carefully avoid the deeper drifts,
The icy patches that might make them slip.

And then I stop and lift the buckets down
And scatter out the cake, pile after pile,
Upon the hard, bare patches free from snow,
And, as I do, insisting all the while,

That each must eat these hearty protein bits,
So full of nourishment. That 'twould be wrong
To fail to do this simple, easy thing
To help an unborn calf grow big and strong.

I check them over with a mother's eye
And watch to see that each one gets her share,
That bold ones do not push the shy aside,
And when my buckets all are emptied bare,

We ruminate together for a while,
Oblivious to the morning's icy sting,
I rub a friendly forehead one more time
And wish them easy calving come next spring.

People sometimes ask us just what we do all day on a ranch.

AN ORDINARY MORNING

'Twas just an ordinary mornin'
Somewhere along in May,
When my husband hollered from the yard,
And then I heard him say,
"I'm goin' to the pasture,
It'll take an hour or two,
And if you'd like to come along,
We'll drive out in Old Blue."

Now I don't get to tag along
Much, as a general rule,
But I'd finished with the chorin'
And the kids were all in school.
'Twould be just like we were courtin'
I was happy at the chance,
For you take it where you find it
When it comes to ranch romance.

Now Old Blue is kind of ancient
And he's got some scars and dents,
'Cause we use him when we're feedin',
Checking cows and fixing fence.

But the engine runs like clockwork,
And the tires are pretty fair,
All except that right front whitewall
That sometimes loses air.

And there's a chunk of baling wire
To fasten down the hood,
And a saddle blanket for the seat
Where the cushion's not too good.
The cab is kind of cluttered up
With stuff we need, that's true,
There's vet supplies and fencing tools,
And ropes and rifles too.

Well, we headed for the pasture
('Course I opened every gate.)
And we found that little heifer,
The one that calved so late.
Her bag was near to bustin'
Milk was dripping' from each teat,
For she'd kick that little feller
Every time he tried to eat.

So my husband said, "I'll fix her
And I'll do it slick as soap,
'Cause I've got you here to help me,
And I brought along my rope.
Now I'll ride Blue on the fender,
And you steer him from the seat,
And I'll rope that little mama
And we'll let her baby eat."

Well, I lined up on that heifer,
And he built himself a loop.
Then she took off at a gallop,
So I just poured on the soup
And Old Blue was doing thirty
When we topped that little knoll,
But he had her caught for certain
--Then I hit that badger hole.

The cow kept right on goin'
But we made a sudden stop.
My husband landed underneath
And Old Blue was there on top.
But I saw that rope come trailin' past,
And it cheered me up a mite,
So I jumped right out and grabbed it,
And I snubbed that critter tight

Around a most convenient rock.
You should have heard her beller.
Then I went lookin' for the calf,
And I brought that little feller
And I held him to his mama,
And it really pleased me some
To see his little belly
Growin' round, just like a drum.

Made me think about my husband.. . . .
So I went back to Old Blue
To kind of take a look around
See what I had to do.
Blue was standin' kind of hip-slung,
'Cause one wheel was up some higher,

But 'twas nothin' that I couldn't fix
With just some balin' wire.

My husband lay there underneath,
Said he thought his leg was broke.
But it made me pretty happy
Just to know he didn't croak,
So I twisted stuff together
And I stuck Blue in reverse
And I backed out of that badger hole.
Then I heard my husband curse;

And when I stopped to think of it,
He was right, without a doubt,
Instead of backin' over him.
I should have pulled him out.
Well, I got him loaded in Old Blue
'Mongst all those other things,
Propped his leg up with that blanket
Though it meant I rode the springs.

And we finally limped on into town,
Not travelin' very fast.
Old Blue, he got new tie rods,
And my husband got a cast.
Just an ordinary mornin'
Really nothin' out of line.
By the way, I checked that heifer
And that calf is doin' fine.

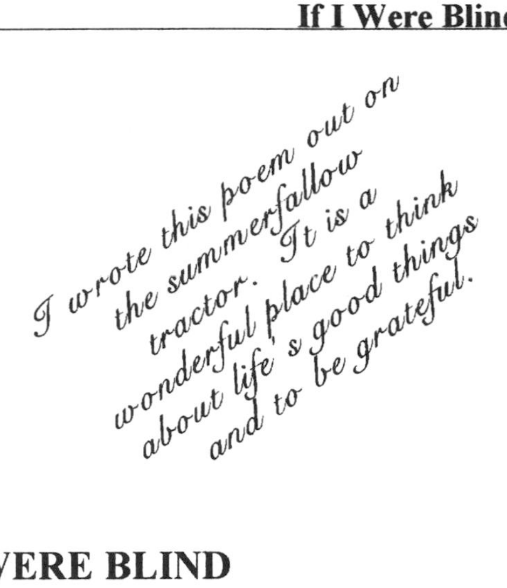

IF I WERE BLIND

If I were blind and could not see the sunrise
  Nor watch the frolicking of calves in spring,
Perhaps I still could feel the sun's caress
  And hear the prairie grasses whispering.

If I were deaf and could not hear a bird's call
  Nor windsong in the rustling aspen trees,
Perhaps I still could sift earth through my fingers
  And catch the scent of roses on the breeze.

But if it were I could not smell the flowers
  Nor feel the texture of a greening leaf,
How sad and narrow would my life be then.
  How deep and unassuagable my grief.

But I've been blessed to know this world about me,
  So blessed to hear and feel and smell and see,
That I am filled with constant awe and wonder:
  How lavish are the gifts God's given me!

You're in cowboy country now.
Prepare for culture shock.
We pray as well to guitar tunes
As we do to Brahms and Bach.

HEAVENLY MUSIC

The deep notes swell, and spread, and soar
To heaven's portals, when an organ plays.
The voices of the Tabernacle Choir
Lift up a hundred strong in hymns of praise.

With slim batons, conductors lead and blend
Orchestral instruments to suit their will
Into one long and glorious paean of joy.
The music's simply wonderful, but still

I think that God himself must start to smile
And angels tap a surreptitious toe,
When cowboys strum a tune on their guitars,
And old-time fiddlers rosin up their bow.

John Wayne has always been my hero, and this poem has the same title as my favorite John Wayne movie.

TRUE GRIT

The crowd had all left the rodeo ground,
Just a bunch of old cowboys were hangin' around.
Hunkered down on rheumatic haunches,
With balding pates and protruding paunches,
Drinkin' to the old days way back when
The horses were tougher and so were the men.
And every time that the jug went 'round
The toasts got longer and more profound.
"Here's to the world's best buckin' horse!"
(That was Tipperary, of course.)
"To the Pony Express that carried the mail!"
"To Old Man Chisholm and his trail!"
To ranchers and rustlers and those in between,
To the rivers they'd crossed and the mountains
they'd seen.

Then old Bill said, with a hearty burp,
"Let's drink to the lawmen--to Wyatt Earp
And Morgan, and Doc, and that OK crew,
They were real brave men, but I'm tellin' you,
The man I remember most of all,
He weren't no real lawman a'tall,

But that fellow from down at the picture show,
The one that had 'True Grit', you know.
I was a lawman once myself.
My guns are at home on the closet shelf,
But if I could ride for the law again
I'd ride in the hoofprints of old John Wayne
When he played that Rooster Cogburn fellow.
Now there was a marshal who wasn't yellow,
With his reins in his teeth and his guns in his hand
He rode right into that outlaw band.
He was old like me, and tired and fat.
I wish I could make one ride like that!"

Then Ed said, "By pure Providence,
There's a horse standin' over along the fence
With a saddle that looks like a pretty good fit
And we're here to judge if you've got true grit.
If you want that ride, you can make it still."
Old Bill stood up. "By God, I will!
But Rooster Cogburn wore a patch,
And so to make it a fairer match
I'll stick my glasses here in my pocket,
Then the ride will be square and you can't knock it;
But when I take 'em off, of course,
You'll have to point me toward that horse.
I was a lawman as you well know,
My guns are at home and I've told you so
But my pickup truck holds a twenty-two
And an old twelve-gauge, and I'll make 'em do!"
So they helped him on and he sat up proud,
Said those famous words and he said 'em loud
And they sounded just like poetry.
Said, "Fill you hands, you S.O.B.!"

Then he stuck the reins into his mouth
And he kicked that horse and they took off south.
He raised up the shotgun and fired a round,
The fellows they all hit the ground
While the pellets riddled the pickup truck
And the horse went into a crow-hop buck.
Bill might have stuck on, as like as not,
He might have stuck on, but he plumb forgot,
Forgot that his teeth were the store-bought kind
And he wore 'em loose so they wouldn't bind.
They slid from his mouth, still chewin' that rein
And Bill came down in a world of pain.

His pocket was filled with shards of glass.
His teeth were scattered across the grass.
His hat was smashed and his Sunday clothes
Were spattered with blood from his busted nose.
But he staggered up--to their vast relief.
Said, "A gritty man don't need no teeth
Nor glasses neither! You know darned well
He can spot a jug by his sense of smell!"
So they passed it around and they had to admit
John Wayne never had no truer grit

And then there are the unsung heroes

HIGH SCHOOL RODEO

They shoved the bulls up into the chutes,
They were big and ugly and fightin' mean,
And the freckle-faced kid who drew number two
Couldn't have been a day over age fifteen.
But he was all business, he wanted to win,
And he wasn't looking to left nor right,
He just studied that hunk of surging flesh
And psyched himself for the coming fight.
He measured off and he took his grip,
And he wrapped his fist with the end of the rope
And eased himself down on that big bull's back.
Then there was nothing but hang and hope.

And somewhere out in the holiday crowd,
Sitting tensely there in the noisy stands,
Clenching her fists 'til her fingernails
Cut bloody slits in the palms of her hands.
Never thinking about the score,
Feeling no shame if he hit the dirt,
Only praying he wouldn't hang up
Or get hooked by a horn, or trampled, or hurt.
And the courage he showed as he nodded his head
And told them to turn that bull outside,
Wasn't any more than the courage shown
By his Mom in the stands who watched him ride.

LH

Most ranch wives have most of the answers to most of the questions most of the time. All you have to do is to ask!

QUESTIONS FOR A RANCH WIFE

How can a woman clean the house,
    And wash and sew and bake,
And be the "go fer" after parts,
    And plow and mow and rake;

And keep the books, and tend the kids
    As only women can,
And still have time to help with chores?
    The unpaid hired man!

The answer's very simple:
    We work real fast, and then
A woman's day has always had
    More hours than those of men.

And in addition, we are kind, generous, loving, and, above all, optimistic. See next poem.

TWO VIEWPOINTS AT WEANING TIME

We weaned the calves today, and we
Sat long upon that fence to see,
Could we discover mid the fuss
Just what the future held for us.

I didn't hear their plaintive bawl,
I didn't see weaning calves at all.
Saw steers and heifers grown and plump
Standing at feed bunks, rump to rump,
Gaining seven pounds a day
On scarcely any grain or hay,
While prices rose so fast, by heck,
We'd be ashamed to cash the check!

But he saw veterinary bills
From calfdom's constant scourge of ills,
Like diarrhea and runny nose,
And he saw waterers that froze,
Tractors broke down from pushing snow
In weather forty-five below,
And silage piles and stacks of hay
That dwindled faster every day;
While prices took a downward slide
'Til calves were scarcely worth their hide.

We sat upon that fence, we two,
Each with a different point of view.
And this will be my prayer each night,
"Oh, Lord, just ONCE let me be right!"

My grandfather was a Quaker, but this is not my grandfather's story.

LONG JOE TAYLOR BAINES

Joe Taylor Baines sat easy on his horse
Peered through the curtain of fresh-falling snow
To catch some telltale movement that would prove
That nesters rode the coulees down below.
The L2 beeves that wintered on this range
Had come up shorter ever since the day
The homesteaders had come to settle here
And somehow someone soon would have to pay.

Joe Taylor Baines stood fully six foot four
And he was called "Long Joe" by those he knew.
Eyes greyer than the Steeldust stud he rode,
Ten years now foreman on the old L2.
He signed on at the ranch a raw green kid
And through the passing years had come to know
The range and cattle like they were his own.
If ever man rode for the brand, 'twas Joe.

A quiet man, he stood a bit apart
And had a Quaker's sense of right and wrong
Perhaps not always kind, but always fair
And honest as a summer's day is long.

He had but one obsession, and that was
To rid the country of that hardy race
Who gambled with the government that they
Could wrest a living from a homestead place.

He held no hatred for them personally.
'Twas only that they did such stupid things
Like plowing good grass under for a field
Or fencing L2 cows away from springs.
He wished they'd take their families and their plows
And for forever leave behind these plains
To cows, like God intended, and to men
Who cared for cattle, like Joe Taylor Baines.

His was no vigilante vengeance, out for blood.
The Quaker way was never using force.
And so he rode these border hills alone,
A grey-eyed watcher on a tall grey horse,
Thinking that could he catch them stealing stock
He could persuade them (such was his belief)
To leave their lands unclaimed, move on, instead
Of facing cowman's justice for a thief.

The grey stud snorted at the rising wind.
Long Joe, as lonely men so often do,
Spoke to his horse, "That storm is coming fast.
I guess we'd best be headin' toward L2."
Back toward "the ranch" - he never called it "home"
He never owned a house, or had a wife.
He had no family ties, no secret loves.
The L2 and the cattle were his life.

And then the grey who never stumbled, slipped.
    His foreleg caught a crevice in the stone,
And as the horse and man fell heavily
    Joe heard the sickening shattering of bone.
He lay a moment, stunned upon the snow,
    Then gingerly he moved his pain-wrenched knee
The grey stud struggled to regain his feet
    And then began to scream in agony.

Forgetful of his own pain, Long Joe turned
    To gaze with horror at protruding bone,
The bloody foreleg dangling uselessly.
    He felt such sorrow he had never known.
He knew the stud would never walk again.
    That there could be for him but one recourse,
He gently stroked the proud grey neck, and then
    Steadied his hand. His one shot killed the
horse.

The wind blew cold. Joe shivered and began
    To weigh the options that were left to him.
Should he make shelter? Try the long walk out?
    He took his knife and whittled on a limb
To form a crutch, tested his knee and counted miles;
    And then the wind brought in a faint "hallo'.
He answered back, the calls came nearer. Then
    The square dark shape that moved through
falling snow

Became a square dark man upon a square
dark horse.
    The old McClellan, laced shoes and
farmer pants

Proclaimed the homestead brand. His quick dark
eyes
Took in Joe's situation at a glance.
"I've seen you riding through these hills," he said.
"That grey horse was a good one, I could tell."
His wry half-smile made Long Joe realize
The watcher had been being watched as well.

"We'd best be moving out before it's dark."
He said no more but with a deft, sure hand
Pulled off the blood smeared saddle from his horse.
Put Long Joe's on, then cinched it tightly, and
With gentle strength he helped Long Joe to mount.
Then saying only, "We've three miles to go."
Shouldered the saddle with its telltale stains.
Caught up the reins and trudged off through the
snow.

The homestead shack was bright and warm within;
The man said, at the woman's startled face,
"I've brought us home some company tonight."
She quickly went to set another place.
The cabin smelled of fresh beef liver, fried,
Of biscuits on a platter, piping hot,
The woman stirred the gravy at the stove,
The coffee bubbled gently in the pot.

The man brushed off the snow and hung their
coats
And helped Joe hobble to a place to sit.
"I'll take you home come morning when it's light,
By then this blizzard should let up a bit.

My horse is much too tired to go tonight,
And, anyway, I think it's time we ate."
The brown eyes met the grey eyes steadily
And Joe reached out and took the proffered plate.

And bowed his head and listened to their prayer.
And as he watched those hungry children eat.
Joe realized that even decent men
Will bend a bit when families need the meat.
And black and white will weave a strange design.
For, can you ever call a man a thief,
When he has saved your life and brought you home
And shared with you his meal of stolen beef?

I WONDERED

Her saddle pants of buckskin gold
Stretched taut across her thighs,
I wondered at which store in town
Stocked britches in that size.

She must have weighed three hundred pounds,
If hat and boots were counted.
I wondered how she would get off.
I wondered how she mounted.

I wondered at the pony who
Would carry such a load.
I wondered at the English way
She posted as she rode.

And when they trotted up the path
As they were exercising,
I wondered why I sudden thought
Of harvest moons arising.

A macho young rancher once told me that I couldn't be a cowboy poet as I wasn't a real cowboy.

OLD BLUE
AND THE PICKUP COWGIRL

I see you look askance and sneer at me
As you ride by upon your fiery steed,
To lope with ease across the grassy plain,
Amaze companions with some roping deed.

Your hat pulled low. Your silver spurs a-jingle.
Your wild rag and your well-worn leather vest.
The Marlboro Man, John Wayne or the Lone
Ranger.
Americana at its very best!

While I jounce slowly in the dusty drags,
The lowliest member of a gallant crew,
For I'm a pickup cowgirl and I ride
A four-wheel mount that's simply called
"Old Blue."

I know at first I loathed my plebeian role,
Demoted and dismounted hurt my pride;
But comes a time when one must face life's facts:
Barefoot and pregnant weren't no way to ride.

Old Blue And The Pickup Cowgirl

So I became a pickup cowgirl, and Old Blue
Was destined to become my favorite mount.
And even though we don't sport spurs and saddle
I dare you say that Blue and I don't count.

We baby-sit the kids while we're out riding;
We bring the water jugs and pack a lunch;
A bunch of posts, a roll of wire and staples,
And it don't take long before I have a hunch

That I'm the one that's going to get to use them.
We haul the dogs when they are in disgrace;
And there are times when someone's city cousin
Comes out to spend a day upon the place.

Just like that fat guy by the name of Clarence,
He only stuck his horse 'til half past ten;
It took two men to lift him from the saddle,
He couldn't walk a single step, so then

I had to take him with me in the pickup.
I don't mind telling you that I was mad.
I begged Old Blue's forgiveness, stomped that throttle,
Hit every bump and ditch that pasture had.

And sometimes when they find a calf that's puny
They stick it in the cab with me to ride,
And when I say a calf is loose, believe me,
I'm not just meaning that his legs ain't tied.

Old Blue and I go back to check the laggards.
We race ahead to count them through a gate.
And in between we do that special job
That wives and pickups do the best--we wait!

And so it hurts me when you sneer at Blue,
More even than the times you laugh at me,
For Blue's got "Ford" across his tailgate and
You can't beat that when talking pedigree.

And there was once when Old Blue saved my life:
We'd gone out just us two to tag some calves.
We'd find a sleeping calf and grazing cow,
Then Blue and I would split that pair in
halves.

And I'd slip out and clamp an eartag in
While Old Blue stood protection at my back.
That critter must have had some race horse blood,
Or maybe I'd just grown a little slack

For she came running when her baby bawled,
All huffied up and feeling full of beans,
I raced her for the pickup, all the while
Her blowing snot and slobber on my jeans.

It was a tie! And both of us jumped in!
That cab just wasn't big enough for two.
I slipped across and out the other door,
Dropped to the ground and bellied under Blue.

She got down on her knees and glared and bellered,
And tried her best to share that little space.
I wasn't winning--still, I hadn't lost yet!
I made an obscene gesture in her face!

She was the most tenacious cow I've ever met.
She circled 'round Old Blue for near two
hours,
Tore up the sod with horn and hoof until
Had I a mind, I could have planted flowers.

But I just lay there, safe as in a church,
The engine dripped some oil on me, of course,
But all that time Blue never moved one wheel.
I'd like to see you try that with your horse!

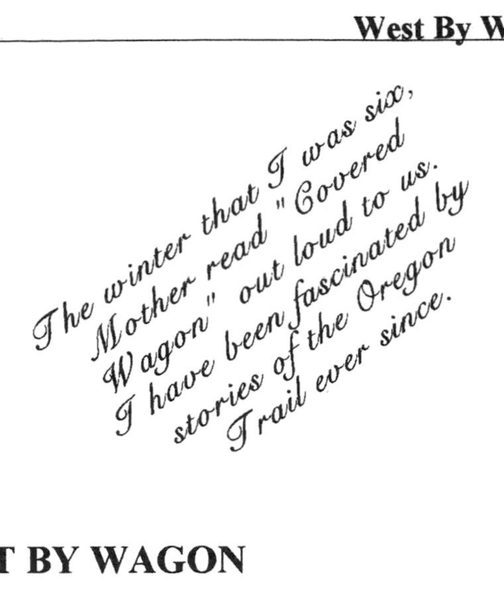

WEST BY WAGON

They were going west by wagon
　　So they rose before the sun;
Each one eager to get started
　　And to get the journey done.
As motley a collection
　　As you'd ever chance to meet,
Driving wheel to wheel with people
　　That they'd snub out on the street.

Some men looking for adventure,
　　Open-eyed at all they saw.
Some men peering sly and furtive,
　　Hiding faces from the law.
In one wagon rode a preacher
　　With a Bible on his knee,
He was off to spread the gospel
　　In that kingdom by the sea.

West By Wagon

Here a rich man's entourage,
All outfitted the best,
Making plans for fame and fortune
And an empire in the west.
Here a couple, gaunt and weary,
Nothing much beside their team
And a wagon full of children,
Just a home was in their dream.

Whether gentleman or scoundrel,
Rich or poor, or cruel or kind.
They had one thing in common:
They had left their pasts behind.
With the dawn upon their shoulders
They were headed for the pass,
For they'd seen the future beckoning
Across the those miles of grass.

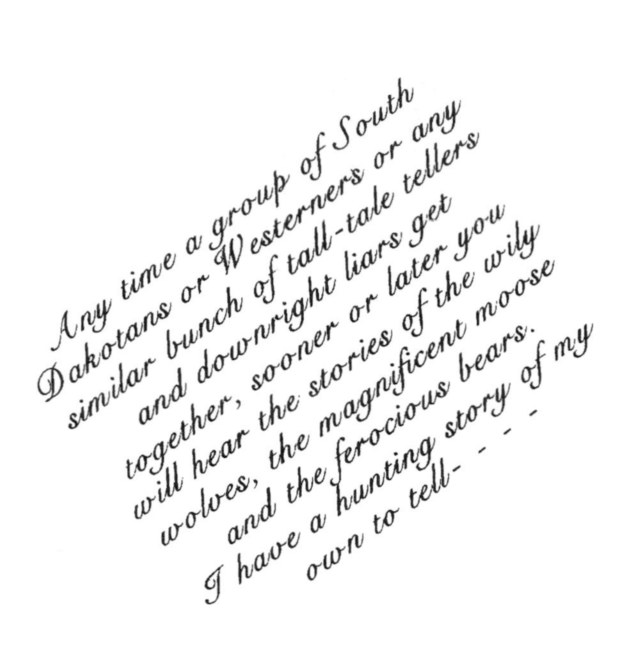

THE LAST GREAT RABBIT HUNT

Back when we first were married
    We were short of cash, and so
We decided we'd hunt rabbits,
    Just to make some extra dough.
Old Sure-Shot with his twenty-two
    And me, the True Believer,
Content to tag along behind
    And act as his retriever.

Those old jacks sure were plentiful,
    We really were in luck
For every four we took to town
    Would bring about a buck.

But we'd not stoop to sell that way,
We thought it would be nifty
To wait to take them 'til we had
Some forty-five or fifty.

Then we'd have a celebration,
Take in a show, no doubt,
A glass of wine, or maybe two,
And we'd have supper out.
So we hunted through the winter
Every chance we got,
For back there in the forties
A dollar meant a lot.

We piled those rabbits on the roof
On the north side of a shed,
And the last time that we tallied
We had a hundred head.
And then the blizzards hit us
And the wind it never stopped.
We shovelled snow and broke the ice
And pitched hay 'til we dropped.

And just as sudden came the sun
And a warm and gentle breeze,
We calved those doggone heifers out
In mud up to our knees.
And on that wind was wafted
Such a stench across the lot
That, finally, we remembered
Those rabbits we'd forgot.

I said, "Today you'll have to haul
Your rabbits out of here."
His most ungallant answer was,
"Those are OUR rabbits, dear!"
And so we made a compromise
And I, with much foreboding,
Said I would load the rabbits up
If he'd do the unloading.

I shinnied up onto the roof
Of that evil smelling shed
And held my breath and shovelled off
Those hundred stinking dead.
And then we took off for the hills
Far from our small abode.
So he could fill his bargain's part
And empty out the load.

I sat there in the pickup
Content I'd done my share,
But minute followed minute
And the rabbits still were there.
I couldn't see him any place
'Til I followed up a hunch,
There, on the ground, my husband lay
A-chucking up his lunch.

Was this the macho hero
That I'd tried so hard to win,
This sorry, sniveling sissy
With the vomit on his chin?

The Last Great Rabbit Hunt

Great was my disillusionment.
I'd really had enough!
I'd show what I was made of,
I'd prove that I was tough!

I jumped into that pickup truck
And grabbed up one big jack,
And fueled by righteous anger
I hurled it out the back.
But, at that very moment,
Above the truck's tailgate
Appeared the sickly visage
Of my wretched, retching mate.

I swear I tried to stay that throw,
I really tried my best,
But that rank and rotten rabbit
Hit him squarely in the chest.
I told him I was sorry
And I tried hard not to laugh,
For the situation's humor
Somehow missed my better-half.

Full forty years have passed and still
These memories make us wince.
Let's close the book. Suffice to say
We've shot no rabbits since!

My Irish grandmothr believed in omens and portents and things that go bump in the night. I don't---exactly-----

OWL'S OMEN

In breathless stillness that occurs
Just before the dawn,
I stare out of my window
Across the dew-wet lawn

To the tall tree where the gray owl
Hoots softly at the night
Then spreads his wings to silent sail
Above the yard in flight.

A round-eyed hunter searching
For small defenseless mice
He sweeps the grass and o'er the house
Not merely once, but twice.

I've heard the gray owl's shadow
Is a harbinger of death
Not just for mice, but man as well.
I draw a frightened breath

And hurry to each sleeper's side
To pray aloud each name.
God must have heard my litany
For morning's all that came.

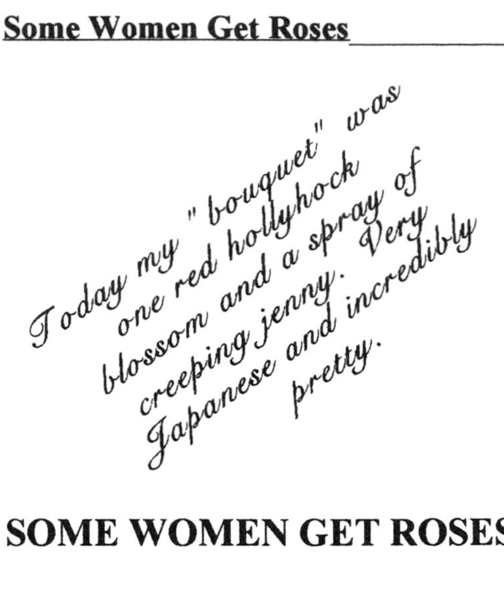

SOME WOMEN GET ROSES

Some women get roses!

Velvet of petal and long of stem,
Placed in a box like a precious gem.
Brought by a man from the florist's place,
Beautifully right for a crystal vase.

I get crocuses!

Only a little bunch of course,
Picked by a man on a saddle horse.
Slightly wilted and (please don't laugh)
Smelling a lot like baby calf.

Some women get orchids!

Pale with a delicate mottled throat,
Made to pin on a sable coat
That is slipped on over a Dior gown
For a ride in a limousine uptown.

I get sunflowers!

Strong and sturdy and bright and bold,
Reflecting the prairie sun's own gold.
I stick them up in my old hat brim
And go for a pickup ride with him.

Now hothouse flowers have their place, I know,
And they're beautiful! But I wouldn't trade
For one bluebell plucked from the morning grass
And, wet with dew, on my pillow laid.

This is our daughter Jonni's
favorite poem.

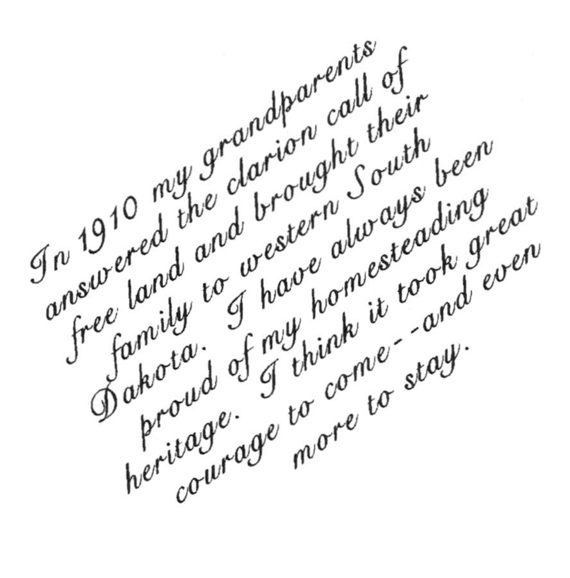

FREE LAND

An empire! One hundred and sixty acres!
Promised free to the eager takers.
A home for their families is what they sought
With plowshares bright as the dreams they brought.
They built their schools and they worshipped God,
And they plowed their furrows in prairie sod.
Then they looked to the sky, but they looked in vain,
For the sky stared back, but it didn't rain.
And the crops soon died and the grass grew sere,
And there was no harvest at all that year.
And some turned their backs and they cursed this land
That had buried their hopes in the windblown sand.

Returned to the east, to the settled land,
To the drudgery of a hired hand;
Back to the life they had always known
And forgot their dreams of a place of their own.

And some kept their faces turned to the west,
Followed the sun o'er the mountain crest,
Wondering if their destiny
Would be found in the mines or down by the sea.

But some of them stayed. Though I do believe
That these were the ones too poor to leave.
They patiently suffered through the drought
They made things do or they did without.
And the summer's sun and the winter's cold
Soon made young people into old.
But somehow from somewhere deep inside
Grew a strange and stubborn sense of pride,
A stoicism that could endure,
A simple faith that was true and pure,
And they learned to love that vast blue sky,
The gray snow clouds that went scudding by,
The gentle promise of April days,
The August sun that could burn and blaze,
The wide clean sweep of open space,
And they made a home from that homestead place.
But all of those homesteaders would agree
That nothing was ever given free.

It is wonderful to wake up at seventy and find life exciting!

MITTEN CHRISTMAS

We called them "Mitten Christmases"
Back there when we were young,
For when the presents all were wrapped
And stockings all were hung,
There'd be no big surprises
For we knew that in each box
Were things we need--like mittens,
And underwear, and socks.
Though grateful for the warmth and love
We longed for some surprise,
Some super-special gift that would
Bring wonder to our eyes.

I thought that growing older
Would be "mitten Christmas" too,
I'd settle for necessities
As people often do.
I'd draw my circle closer
Be grateful for old friends,
Forget about the dreams of youth,
Make do with what life sends.
But a gracious heavenly Santa Claus
Gift-wrapped some verse for me,
And I am like the child who finds
A bike beneath the tree.

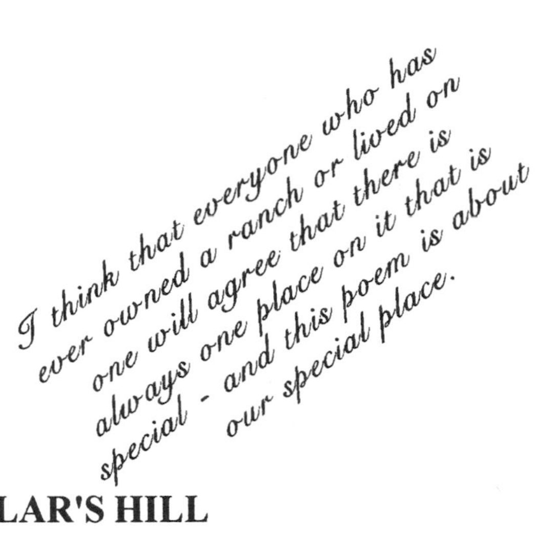

COLLAR'S HILL

We bought the quarter forty years ago
Because it joined our home place on the east.
'Twas mostly hill, a high and rocky dome,
But there would be some grazing there at least.

Reason enough to purchase any ground.
We never thought we bought it for the view
(That's not the way a rancher pays his bills.)
But now I guess we must confess 'twas true.

Whenever folks come to our place to stay,
It's out to Collar's Hill we always go
To see the graves beneath their cairns of stone,
The teepee rings that circle down below.

We gaze across the grasslands and the fields,
Like patches on some old-time crazy quilt,
And count along the creeks eight spots of blue,
The pasture dams my husband staked and built.

And ten miles south across the Grand we'll see
The ridge of bluffs that's always been
"The Wall,"
And farther yet, along the skyline's edge,
A single butte stands sentinel and tall.

And if we stay until the darkness falls,
From forty miles away we'll see a light,
The street lamps of a little prairie town,
A glow of reassurance in the night.

"Why do you call it 'Collar's Hill' ?" folks ask.
"The land is yours, no matter whose it was."
And so we try to make them understand
It will be always "Collar's Hill" because

He was the first to own it; it was here
He came to homestead eighty years ago.
We've tried recalling what we've heard of him
But there is really little that we know.

He stayed just long enough to prove his land;
He had no wife or children at his side;
No one still lives who knows from whence he came,
Or where he went, or how or when he died.

Three things we do recall that we've been told.
No litany of virtues or of faults:
He had a big mustache, he paid his bills,
And, oh, how beautifully that man could waltz.

We've walked the land where once his buildings
stood,
No boards remain, no broken bits of things,
One square of rock, foundation for his house,
And scattered near it are the teepee rings

Where Indians had camped some time before.
The circles lay complete, untouched there still,
Where they had stopped to rest awhile and mourn
The dead that they had buried on the hill.

I wonder if he thought of them as friends,
If lithe brown maids on slender deer-skinned
feet
Waltzed with him in the dusty grass of dreams
To measured one-two-three of tom tom beat.

Somehow this hill became our special place
And Mr. Collar like some long-gone friend.
We climbed his hill to watch a rose-gold dawn,
Hiked rain-soaked grass to find a rainbow's
end.

And every spring, we hurried forth to pluck
From melting snow along the southern slope,
The purple pasques--or crocus, if you will--
Those first brave little harbingers of hope.

And when the northern lights blazed in the sky
And fully half the heavens were aglow,
We listened to celestial music there,
Like static on some ancient radio.

And many a winter Sunday afternoon,
We climbed with kids, made forts among the drifts,
And rows of angels in the clean white snow,
And left them there as offerings and gifts.

Butt-slid in waltz-time down that rocky slope
In gay procession like a flock of geese,
Trudged home at dusk in cold and sodden clothes,
Exhausted, bruised, and aching, but at peace.

And when the Perseids rode wild
At midnight on a sultry August night,
We spread our blanket on the dry brown grass
And watched those meteors fill the sky with light.

So thank you, Mr. Collar, for your hill.
It's scarcely paid its way in graze, that's true,
But it has grown a crop of memories
And no one with a soul can fault the view.

And when I climb that last and final hill,
A higher one than this I hope 'twill be
Where angels play a day-long golden song,
Please, Mr. Collar, save one waltz for me.

This poem is about a sorry sort of a ranch kid. However------

WILLIE

Willie'd never make a cowboy
'Least there didn't seem much hope;
He couldn't stick a bucker
And he couldn't throw a rope.

He couldn't cut a heifer out,
He couldn't man the chute,
And when he held the vaccine gun
Only God knew who he'd shoot.

He backed into the branding fire
He dallied round his thumb
And all those other cowboys
Thought Willie sure was dumb.

About the sorriest cowpoke
Who ever hit the West.
For work was hard for Willie
Talk was what he did best.

And they all figured he'd become
Just an educated fool
When Willie left the ranch behind
To spend some time in school.

But Willie has come home again
        And Willie's coining cash.
He wears a big black Stetson
        And a handlebar mustache.

His boots are alligator
        And the tops come up knee-high;
Has a fringy leather jacket
        And a great big bolo tie.

His pickup's chrome-encrusted
        'Til the dazzle hurts your eyes.
Matches with that silver buckle
        That is almost hub cap size.

And Willie has big bucks to spend
        In bars on babes and beer
And he makes it all just talking--
        Willie's now an auctioneer!

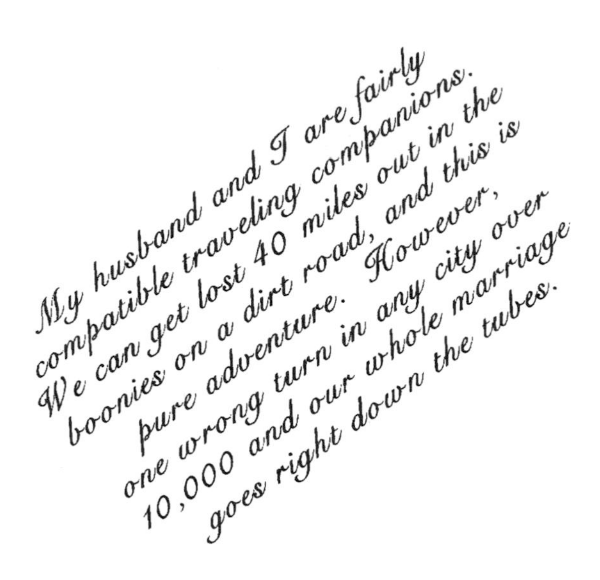

GOING THROUGH CALGARY

We'd been on a trip, just the two of us,
For almost a month without a fuss.
We were sailing along like a southbound breeze
To Calgary from Lake Louise.
I was driving our diesel van
And he had the map, so he could plan
And easy route, if one could be found,
That would take us through, or with luck, around
CALGARY.

Going Through Calgary

He studied that map and he read and he read,
And I drove and I drove and I finally said,
"This traffic is getting thicker and thicker,
We really have no time to dicker.
We just passed Exit 58
And this one's Rolling Hills Estate.
Give some instructions soon to me
Because we now are definitely
AT CALGARY."

He scratched his head and adjusted his cap,
And looked once more at his Canada map.
Said, "You could stay on 1 or switch to 2
But either will take you right into
DOWNTOWN CALGARY.

"Or you could take 22 to 4
And keep on the edge a little more,
Or, if you took 23 on down,
It would take you clear around the town
TO SWEETGRASS."

"But," he said, "You're a little late!
You should have taken Exit 58!
You really did mess up on that!
Now I guess you're headed for Medicine Hat
OR MOOSE JAW!"

Right there our vacation went to pot.
My collar started feeling a little hot.

And if I weren't a lady through and through,
I'd have told that man what he could do
WITH MOOSE JAW!

As it was, I said, "An alligator
Would be a better navigator.
At least he'd keep us headed south!"
The words were hardly from my mouth
When he said, "Since you know it all!"
And he wadded that map in a little ball
And threw it into the back of the van.
And there I was, without a plan
IN CALGARY!

Well, there was nothing else to do,
So I stayed on 1 and we made it through.
In fact, it wouldn't have been half bad
If I hadn't been so doggone mad.
For the next fifty miles neither one of us spoke,
Then, somehow, we started to see the joke
And both of us began to laugh.
So now me and my better-half
Have planned another trip next June---
A sort of second honeymoon--
TO SWEETGRASS!

Wind is one of the facts of life in South Dakota

DAKOTA WIND

The wind that's born on mountain tops,
On desert wastes or far-off seas,
When reaching the Dakota plains
Will blow perversely as it please.

The breeze that brings the scent of flowers,
Caresses the emerging grain,
Will change to tempest overnight,
Chill down new calves in icy rain.

And on a cold clear winter night
This devil wind that has no form
Will slide the snow insidiously
'Til it becomes a raging storm.

The cooling draft that brings relief
To fitful sleepers in July,
Will cease for days, no windmills turn
And all the watertanks go dry.

Wind gently ripples ripening wheat
Or carves a dustbowl in the sod.
It blows unfettered, ever free,
And knows no master--only God.

Our hometown of Thunder Hawk was named for a Sioux chief. He is buried nearby on the Grand River.

INDIAN SCOUT

He slithered stealthily along the bluff,
  Took off his hat and tousled up his hair,
And bellied over to the edge to peer
  Between the stems of sagebrush growing there.
The Indian encampment lay below
  Half-circled by the slow and muddy Grand,
And by the painted lodges he could tell
  'Twas old Chief Thunder Hawk's own band.

Old Thunder Hawk, the fiercest of the Sioux,
  No braver chief, nor wilier a foe
E'er led his tribe across Dakota land.
  And there'd be dancing in that village down
    below
As soon as darkness clothed the prairie hills,
  (The sun was setting; it would not be long.)
For somewhere in those teepees, under guard,
  Bound tightly hand and foot with rawhide thong,
His best friend, Red, they'd ridden many a mile,
  And then the Kid, poor gangling, frightened Kid,
And grizzled old John Blake who would not flinch
  At anything those savage redskins did.

Captured this morning, he alone escaped,
  And he must rescue them or they would die.
He knew that they would do the same for him,
  And though it cost his life, he still must try.

Ft. Pierre lay to the east two hundred miles,
  The cavalry was somewhere in between,
But they could never reach this place in time
  If he could find them on that sea of green.
The hounds began their shrill cacophony,
  One swarthy brave stepped out to scan the sky
And all the bluffs along the river's edge.
  Could he escape that piercing eagle eye?
He must think quickly, must devise some plan.
  He hunkered lower, held his breath---and then
His Mother called, "It's time for supper, son!"
  And Indian Scout was little boy again!

While driving home from Montana, my husband made a rather obscene remark about some sheep we passed, and I thought about what he would have been like had he lived in the days of the sheep and cattle wars.

OLD COWMAN

He was a big man like the hills and sky,
Compassion felt for all who crossed his path
Except one breed of man and beast who faced
His bitter anger and unyielding wrath.

He hated sheep--and sheepmen! That was fact.
No variation in degree or if deserved.
He loathed the herders and he swore the dogs
Were far more human than the men they
served.

"The cowmen blazed the trails and made them safe
And everything was fine," he'd say, "until
Those dad-blamed woollies came a-sneakin' in,
Like vultures to somebody else's kill."

"They ate the grass clean down into the roots,
And then they pulled the roots out of the
ground.
No self-respecting cow would ever drink
From waterholes that sheep had been around."

Old Cowman

He liked long rides and drinking campfire coffee,
And blankets spread beneath a starry sky.
He thought a man who lived cooped in a wagon
Might just as well crawl in his grave and die.

He said that cows were smart and self-sufficient,
While sheep were stupid and they stunk,
besides,
And even dead cows served a useful purpose--
You made your boots and saddles from their
hides.

In town and dining fancy, T-bone steak
Three inches thick was all he'd ever eat.
He viewed a minted lamb chop with disdain,
"Real men didn't put no panties on their
meat!"

He daily spoke with God as to a friend.
Believed in Heaven's glory and Hell's fire.
We wondered if he'd read the Shepherd's Psalm
But dared not ask lest we should raise his ire.

We knew he'd never change nor compromise.
Across the western plains old feuds run deep.
He swore that cows were rightful heirs to grass.
"Them baa-baa-bastards" what he called
the sheep.

I am awed by the courage of the women who came to settle the west. Sometimes waiting is the hardest job of all.

STORE CANDY

"Don't go," she said. "We'll do with what we have."
She knew her words would be to no avail,
He never understood her strange, fey fears
Of spectral things that lurked beside the trail.
She'd seen them in the storm the night before
And though the wind had hushed now and the snow
No longer slid in sibilant whispers, still she knew
That they were waiting. "Please don't go!"

"The weather'll hold," he said. "Our son will have
Store candy in his stocking Christmas morn,
And we'll keep Christmas as it should be kept.
Santa must ride!" He left her there forlorn.
She watched the horse and rider disappear,
Her nervous fingers plucked her apron fold,
The whistled notes of "Jingle Bells" came back
Like icy echoes in the still, clear cold.

Store Candy

All day she worked as though she were possessed.
She nursed the babe and saw their son was fed.
She scrubbed and polished 'til the cabin shone.
She baked the pies and mixed the Christmas bread
And hung the decorations on the tree--
Small crafted things tied on with bright yarn
strands
And to their son's delight, she sat and cut
Long chains of paper angels holding hands.

The sundogs danced the weary sun to rest,
She lit the lamp and still he wasn't there.
She hung the stockings up beside the fire,
She tucked the children in and said a prayer
And then she waited, watching by the window,
The eerie lights were flaring across the
northern sky.
And she waited, listening, only hearing
The old clock tick the anxious minutes by.

He rode the trail hunched up against the cold,
Intent on reaching home before the night.
His saddlebags bulged out like Santa's pack.
He did not see the shadow, white on white,
That sat upon the bank. The long ears twitched,
The haunches crouched to spring in quick
retreat,
The snow crust broke. The frightened rabbit slid,
Flailing in terror, beneath the horse's feet.

The startled horse lashed out. He slipped and fell.
He rose to run and crash into a tree.

The low-hung branches caught the rider hard,
 The saddle turned, the man did not fall free
But foot through stirrup, in cold, stiff leather hung,
 Unconscious and unknowing from the shock,
He dragged behind that frantic, headlong flight
 Across the iron-hard waste of brush and rock
Until at last the horse steadied himself,
 Retraced his way back to the trail to stand
Head down and patient, waiting for the man
 To rise, and mount again, and take command.

The blood pooled red and froze upon the snow;
 The man moved not nor did he draw a breath.
Night shadows crept across the quiet hills,
 Then there was only darkness, cold and death.
A coyote cried from up along the ridge,
 The horse pawed nervously, began to take
Slow, sidewise steps down that long trail
 toward home,
 Dragging the inert body in his wake.

She heard them coming down along the trail,
 She grabbed her coat and lantern and she flew
Outside to meet him, holding high the light.
 She looked but once, and then she knew---
 she knew
That he was far beyond her power to aid.
 There was no one on earth could help him now,
And she alone must do what must be done.
 She could not leave the children anyhow;

Nor could she bring that broken thing inside;
For their small sakes she must keep
Christmas Day;
And so she dragged him down into a stall
And laid him gently on a pile of hay.
Then slipping back into the house, she knelt,
Drew from its hiding place beneath their bed,
Her Christmas gift to him, a patchwork quilt
She'd sewed in secret and she'd tied in red
Because he liked bright colors. She covered him,
Smoothed the quilt carefully, and as she
turned to go
She stumbled on one snowy saddlebag.
She opened it with fingers stiff and slow;

And gazed upon the sacks of Christmas sweets.
The lantern flared and flickered, and it seemed
The shadows drew in closer, taunted her,
Reached boldly out to grasp her, and
she screamed
And screamed, and in blind terror took the candy
By the handfuls, the gaudy green and red,
And threw it at those dancing shapes until
The saddlebag was empty. Then she fled
Into the house and shut and locked the door
And leaned against it, too spent to even cry,
Stared vaguely 'round the room until
Those two small empty stockings caught
her eye.

She slowly filled them up with homemade sweets
   And little gifts, then sat there cold and numb
Until their son awoke with joyous cries
   That Santa Claus had really, truly come.

And she kept Christmas, all that endless day,
   And all the next, 'til punchers riding back
From holiday carousal in the town
   Read out the story written in the track,
They saw the hat, the broken branch, the blood,
   And followed that grim trail until they found
The battered corpse beneath the patchwork quilt,
   And all the bright store candy scattered 'round.

An eastern lady wrote to tell me that she had spent a whole day on a S.D dude ranch, where she had "experienced the cowboy life style" and "ridden free."

RIDING FREE

It seems each drug store cowboy
    And each rhinestone wanna-be
Extols the virtues of the West
    And the joys of "Riding Free."
They'll trot out in the summer,
    But just on sunny days,
On gentle nag with rented tack
    To watch the cattle graze.

They'll eat a catered luncheon
    And often stop to rest,
And think they are experiencing
    The life style of the West.
And 'round a blazing campfire
    While the moon peaks o'er the bluff,
They will state with bland assurance
    That "ranching ain't so tough!"

I'd like to see them out here
When it's thirty-five below
With a northwest wind a-whistling
And piling up the snow,
Trying to get the cattle fed
And sheltered from the blast
With the sick, gut-wrenching knowledge
That the stacks are dwindling fast.
Or watch them tired and dragging
From calving midnight hours,
Or see their shocked expression
When they're treating calves with scours.

Or when the creeks are drying up
And the sun is glaring down,
And rain is just a memory
And the pastures burnt and brown.
When taxes and the feed bills
Are keeping you from sleep,
Or when calves are fat and frisky
But the price is too darned cheap.
When life just isn't turning out
Like movies that you see,
I'd like to ask those fellows then
If this is "Riding Free."

But when I've finished whining
And all complaints are made,
I'll have to be plumb honest
And admit I wouldn't trade
With any city slicker
Or suburbanite elite,

Riding Free

Who punches clocks at nine and five
        And walks a crowded street,
Who locks his doors and locks his heart
        To keep his neighbors out.
I'll tally up the pros and cons
        And know without a doubt
That I'm doing what I want to do.
        I'm where I want to be.
And I guess, when all's considered,
        You could call that "Riding Free."

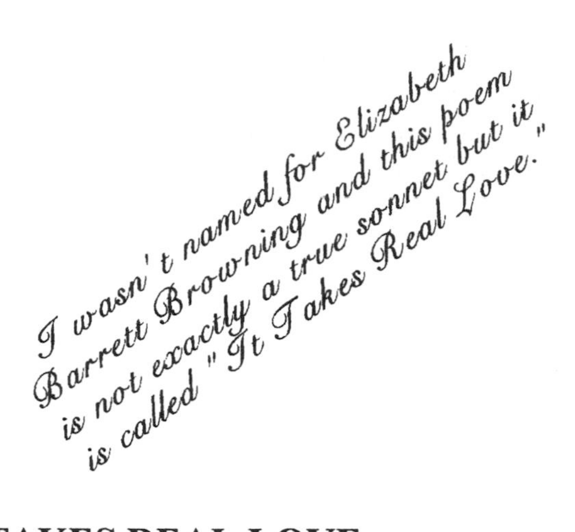

IT TAKES REAL LOVE

It takes real love to kiss a man
Whose whiskers poke and scratch,
Whose morning breath smells just like eggs
--Last year's that didn't hatch.

It takes real love to kiss a man
In cattle-checkin' clothes,
Who used his sleeve to wipe the calf
And then to wipe his nose.

But there is one situation
Where real love is not enough,--
You never never kiss a man
Whose lip is filled with snuff!

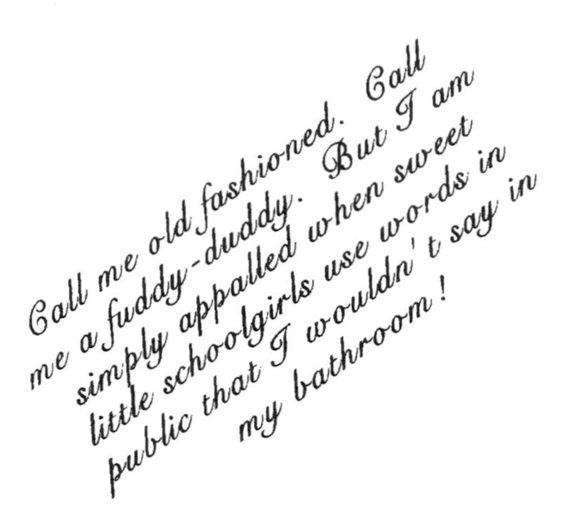

FOUR LETTER WORDS

In these days of women's liberation,
Some modern females across this nation
Use four-letter words with ease and unction
To delineate each bodily function,
While I, with my cheeks a scarlet blaze,
Search for some euphemistic phrase.

It's really not that I'm such a prude,
Though I do consider some words quite crude,
But I remember my childhood days
And a mother with proper Quaker ways
Who, when one of these four-letter slips
Glibly passed my adolescent lips,
Used a four-letter word of her own to cope,
And my tongue still tingles from taste of SOAP!

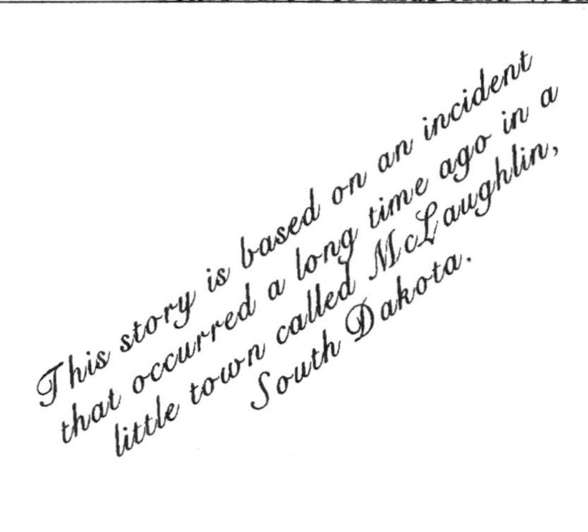

TEARS ARE FOR KIDS AND WOMEN

"Tears are for kids and women," he was told.
"If ridin' bulls is how you aim to go
You'd better learn to tough it out and grin,
There ain't no cryin' time in rodeo!"

The bulls were in his blood when he was born
He cut his teeth on poddy milk cow calves,
Then yearling steers would feel his raking spurs.
He never did do anything by halves

And when he hit that ground so doggone hard
That pain would juice his baby blues all wet
He'd wipe his face off on his dusty sleeve
And swear to God that it was only sweat.

He studied bulls and riders, tried to learn
The whys and wherefores of the things they did.
The old hands gladly passed their lore on down,
It wasn't hard to like that gritty kid.

He lost his share. There ain't no easy way.
But bucked off hard and hurtin' bad as sin,
He'd wipe his face off on his dusty sleeve,
And cuss a bit, and kick the dirt, and grin.

The day was hot with portent of a storm.
The sweat was drippin' off the pickup men.
The chute boss eyed the clouds with wary eyes.
The stock was movin' nervous in the pen.

The kid had drawn a bull they called "Old Top"
A whirling dervish in a yellow hide.
But if you stuck until the whistle blew
He'd guarantee you'd make a winning ride.

Old Top was spinning when he left the chute
The kid was brushed off balance by the gate,
Hung up somehow and swept into that whirl
Whose vortex was a ton of yellow hate.

They heard the crack of hoof on human bone,
They heard the last thin gurgle of his breath.
They jerked him free and lured Old Top away,
And he lay in the dust, alone with Death.

He never heard the whistle when it blew.
He never did find out that they had lied.
But back behind the chutes, all unashamed,
Old cowboys cussed, and kicked the dirt--
and cried.

I realized a long time ago that I would never win a Good Housekeeping award. Probably because, though I was taught how to read a book when I was four, no one ever taught me how to lay one down.

MOLLY'S HOUSE

Molly's way of keeping house
 Is different from mine,
Molly has a model home,
 See how the windows shine.
Molly's husband goes to work
 In ties and tailored suits.
My husband runs his business here
 In jeans and cowboy boots.

Molly has some rare antiques,
 They're priceless, I've been told.
My furniture is not so rare,
 But I'll guarantee it's old.
I've well-read volumes piled around
 Everywhere you look.
Her library consists of
 One coffee-table book.

But Molly has no chipping paint,
No footprints on her floor.
Each picture's framed and matted
Just to match the rooms decor.
I have refrigerator art
And on some the paint's still damp.
But each artist signed her picture
"With love to Gram and Gramp."

A shining silver tea set
Rests on Molly's breakfast bar.
My countertop has lots of crumbs
And a half-full cookie jar.
Molly's dinners are divine
A perfect gourmet treat.
Somehow my menus seem to run
To plain old spuds and meat.

Sometimes I envy Molly's house,
Its polish and its shine.
But when it comes to living there
-- I think I'll stick with mine.

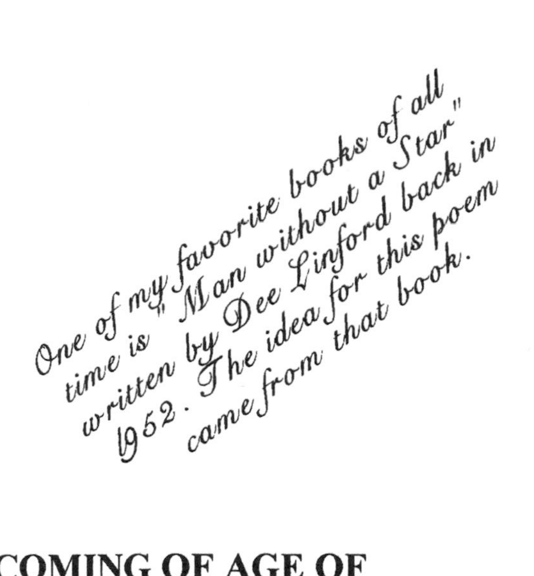

THE COMING OF AGE OF BILLY BRADDOCK

Young Billy Braddock was just a stray,
He came riding into the ranch one day
With a ragged shirt upon his back
And not much more tied up in a sack,
On a horse gone lame and traveling slow,
Both gaunted down 'bout as far as they'd go.

"Company comin'" yelled the cook
And the boss went out to take a look
And kind of size up what he saw--
Too young to be runnin' from the law,
Must have had a fight with his paw,
'Cause something about the set of his jaw
Reminded the boss how, years before,
His own dad had kicked him out the door.

So the boss said, "Howdy. Light and eat."
And to the kid the words were sweet,
And sweeter still when he added, "And
If you're needin' a job, I'm needin' a hand."

So Billy bunked in with the rest of the crew,
And they all hoorawed him as cowboys do
With rough good humor and rustic wit.
The boss was pleased that he didn't quit,
For Billy was chosen as pilot, of course,
He could "pile it" out from the stabled horse,
Was sent on fool's errands that made him late,
Was left behind to shut every gate;
It was frog in the boot, and snake in the bed,
The gun that went off right over his head,
And the gentle old mare who bucked real bad
When a cactus was stuck in her saddle pad.

But the one thing that they always did
That really rankled was call him "Kid."
And exclude him from their company
When they rode to town for their payday spree.
Sayin' a child with a peach-fuzz face
Just didn't belong in that wicked place,
And they'd take him along someday, perhaps,
When he grew out of diapers and into chaps.

Billy took their ribbing with fair good grace
And for six full months never left the place.
But the very next time payday came 'round
Billy got in line and he stood his ground,

Said, "I'm takin' my money, too, and then
I'm ridin' to town with the rest of the men."
The boss kind of hated to see him go
But he'd earned his wage and he couldn't say "No."

So Billy took his turn at the water trough,
Shaved a few downy whiskers off,
Brushed the dirt from his only coat,
Tied a clean bandanna around his throat,
Mounted his horse, pulled his hat well down
And rode with the others into town.

Came a whoopin' in off that dusty trail,
Threw his reins 'round the hitchin' rail
And busted right through that swingin' door
(Though he'd never been in a saloon before).
Bellied up to the bar with the rest of the boys,
Eager to sample the dubious joys
Of rotgut whiskey and crooked games
And first encounters with dance hall dames.

Said, "Whatever they're drinkin', I'll have one too."
But he kind of gagged on the potent brew,
And everyone knew as he choked it down
That another sucker had come to town.
But Bill was a man among the men,
So he emptied his glass again and again
'Til the room was afloat in a smoky haze
Through which he walked in a drunken daze,

And when poker playin' time came 'round
He couldn't tell his ace from a hole in the ground,

So the dealer didn't even have to cheat
To guarantee that Bill'd be beat.

Now a barroom floozie whose name was Bea
Came and perched on Billy's knee
Cast a practiced eye on his dwindling store,
(She was twice his age and a little more)
Her satin dress was a sleazy green
And her neck and her elbows weren't too clean,
But she kissed his cheek and she stroked his hair
And he stumbled after her up the stair.

Young Billy Braddock rode out of town,
Shoulders hunched and his hat pulled down,
Same trail he'd ridden in yesterday,
Nothin' to show for six months pay
But a head like a hive full of angry bees
And a darned good case of a social disease.

I regret to admit it
but the modern cowgirl
has her stressful
moments also.

LADY IN THE CORRAL

She arises Sunday morning
　　　　And off to church she goes,
Dressed in the latest fashion,
　　　　High heels and silken hose.
She smiles and murmurs pleasantries
　　　　"Til the service starts, and then
She sings a sweet soprano
　　　　Comes in clear with her "Amen."

A perfect lady you would say
　　　　If you saw her on a Sunday,
But what happens to this lady
　　　　When she's working cows on Monday?
She's wearing jeans and cowboy boots;
　　　　She still is looking good,
But the language that she uses
　　　　Just shocks the neighborhood.

Lady In The Corral

She goes to cut a heifer out,
          She spurs into the crush,
And the names she calls that heifer
          Would make a sailor blush.
A bull begins to bellow
          And to cut some bullish capers.
The lineage she assigns to him
          Is not what's on his papers.

The men all stare in disbelief
          But it's not as bad by half
As the phrases that she'll formulate
          When she's working on a calf.
But, come next Sunday morning,
          She'll be all sweet and pure
For she leaves those words where they belong
          Out there with the manure!

I think the world's most nostalgic words are "Home for Christmas."

I WANT AN OLD-TIME CHRISTMAS

Some folks go south for Christmas
　　　Where soft, warm breezes blow.
Give me an old-time Christmas
　　　I want one white with snow!
A hustling, bustling, busy time;
　　　A cold, clear holiday,
With half a hundred things to do
　　　And guests upon their way.

The house will smell of turkey,
　　　Of spices and of pine.
There'll be excited greetings,
　　　And a festive glass of wine.
And no matter what the number,
　　　We'll make room and some to spare;
We'll just crowd a little closer.
　　　Then we'll bow our heads in prayer

For food and friends and family.
　　　"God bless us, every one!"
"Will someone pass the turkey, please?"
　　　"I'd like another bun."

The stuffing, squash and gravy
Will go 'round the laden board.
The salads, pickles, cranberries,
Until with one accord,

We'll eye the pie with longing,
But then we'll have to say,
"Not now! I'll eat mine later."
Then we'll clear the food away
And we'll have some entertainment,
With no generation gap
For everyone will join right in,
And we'll laugh and cheer and clap.

There'll be stories, games and music:
"Jingle Bells" and "Deck the Halls"
While we're munching on the cookies,
Homemade fudge and popcorn balls.
Then the room will grow more quiet
And we'll speak of bygone years,
Remembering folks with laughter
And a sprinkling of tears.

And we'll build a bridge of memories
Back fifty years or so.
Give me an old-time Christmas.
I want one white with snow!

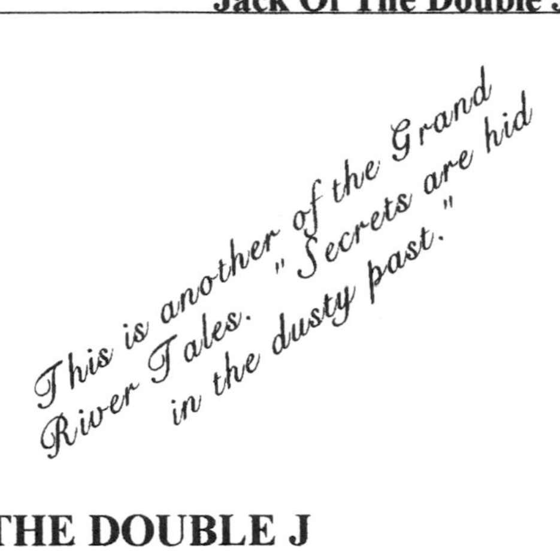

JACK OF THE DOUBLE J

There was a rancher whose name was Jack,
He started out in a cottonwood shack
With next to nothing, and he built him a herd,
For he was a man as good as his word;
And he branded them all with a Double J,
For he was living for the day
He'd marry that girl and he'd bring her there
With her laughing eyes and her long, long hair.
And he did it, just as he said he would.
And she loved him deeply and life was good.
And there through a year of wind and weather
She kept her man and the ranch together.

Now the winter was easy for the grass was prime,
And in the spring about calving time
When the cottonwood trees their leaves unfurl,
She bore him a healthy baby girl
And Jack named her Judith, after her Maw.
Now here fate found his dreams one flaw,
For the baby scarcely once had cried
When her mother closed her eyes and died.

Now Jack looked out at that greening hill
And for a moment he felt his world stand still.
But Jack knew that death was a part of life,
So he picked up his shovel and he buried his wife;
And he picked up his daughter and he buried his
pride,
And he took her east to her mother's side
Of the family--just for a couple of years--
Then he hurried back west to hide his tears,
Back to his horse and his herd and the land
And the cross on the hill with the Double J brand.
For a man must do what a man must do,
And he knew that somehow he'd see it through.

And so Jack worked like a man possessed
Through the long dark days with little rest,
For he hated the nights when the house was still,
Though the neighbors rallied as neighbors will.
But grief is hard for a man to share,
So he built for the daughter who wasn't there.
And the months crept by as they always will,
And the winters weathered the cross on the hill.
Jack labored on and he built his herd.
He never went east but he kept his word
And he sent the checks for his daughter's keep,
And he never complained that the price was steep,
Or even mentioned he thought it strange.
That much would keep ten kids here on the range.

If the winters were hard or beef was low
And the banker was in for as far as he'd go,

Jack hitched up his belt a notch or two
And somehow or another the checks went through.
And every year from spring to fall
A gentle horse stood in the stall
Hoping she'd come. But she never did.
The horse was used by the neighbor's kid
Who came by often in the hope
That Jack would teach him how to rope,
For Jack was known as the best hand
In all that section of the land.

And slowly, slowly the years crept past.
Graduation came at last.
Jack didn't go. When you seldom get to town,
You don't seem to fit with a cap and gown.
But he scoured across the countryside
For a horse like her mother used to ride.
And he and his hands fixed up the place
With carpeted floors and curtains of lace.
A far cry from that cottonwood shack!
A home for a princess coming back!
But she didn't come. I guess you can't
When you're something called a debutante!

But the neighbor's kid always seemed to know
Whenever Jack was feeling low,
And he came riding past that way
And they took their horses and spent the day
Checking fences and cleaning springs,
And talking of simple, mundane things
Like grass and cattle and late spring snows,
And ropes and rigging and rodeos.

In less than a year a message came
That Judith was going to change her name.
Jack didn't go, for cowboy boots
Didn't seem to fit in with swallowtail suits.
But he sent a check, or so they say,
Worth half the steers on the Double J.
And he wandered up to the weathered cross
To mourn awhile this double loss,
The wife who had died and left him lone,
And the daughter that he had never known.

And the neighbor's kid came riding there
With sorrow a thing that they could share.
For his mother had died just the week before,
And he grieved for her, and his heart was sore.
Each ignored the tear in the other's eye
For out in the West grown men don't cry.
But they rode the river trail that day
And though they didn't have much to say,
The warm handclasp at that day's end
Told the kid that Jack was his best friend.

Now like tumbleweeds the years rolled by,
And old Jack died as we all must die.
They found him there with some flowers in his hand,
Up by the cross with the Double J brand.
And the neighbors came to weep and pray
Over two graves under the Double J.
But when the folks back east did hear,
There wasn't one of them shed a tear.
They said, "The old man's finally dead.
We hear he's gathered quite a spread.

What we will do is sell that land,
Sell everything with a Double J brand,
Every acre and every beast
And bring the money all back East."
That's what they thought they'd do until
The lawyer fellow read the will,
And what a man should do is what Jack did
--He left the ranch to the neighbor's kid.

There still would be some more to this tale
If we could follow an old, old trail,
But an untrodden path grasses over fast
And secrets are hid in the dusty past.
Now dead are the only two who'd remember
That terrible blizzard in mid-December
When the neighbor's cattle were all up the creek,
And he and his hands were out for a week
Trying to get them back together.
Jack rode by their ranch in that stormy weather.
But a western blizzard wipes out all tracks-
Now only God knows that kid was Jack's.

Sometimes when it feels
as though the world is crowding in,
I can empathize with the
old-time cowboys.

AN OLD COWBOY'S PRAYER

I never thought too much about Heaven, Lord,
I know it must be nice 'cause You are there,
But I'm afraid those angels flyin' round,
All playin' on their golden harps, might scare
This spooky bronc of mine. I just
Can't stick 'em in the way I used to, God,
And comin' down upon Your golden street
Would be a harder place than prairie sod.

And if it's true that there will be no night.
The way it's written for us in Your Word,
I'd miss the campfires glowin' in the dark,
And when, if ever, would we bed the herd?

And all those fancy people up there, Lord,
My cussin' and my chewin' wouldn't suit,
And so I'm askin' when my time is up
To spend hereafter on some grassy butte
Where I can spot a maverick steer or two,
And hear the killdeers callin' up the rain,
And watch You light that first faint evenin' star
With twilight comin' fast across the plain.

I wish that I could assimilate knowledge as easily as I assimilate calories

TOMORROW'S THE DAY

Tomorrow's the day that I will begin
A diet that's promised to make me thin.
And I will lose all this matronly blubber,
Turn into a swinger instead of a scrubber.
All night I will trip the light fantastic
In hose NOT made of support elastic,
Sit lightly astride a galloping horse,
And drive men mad..(old men, of course).
Yes, tomorrow's the day that the fat will melt
And I will be chic and sleek and svelte.

Alas, through the years I have learned to my sorrow
I always start my diets TOMORROW!

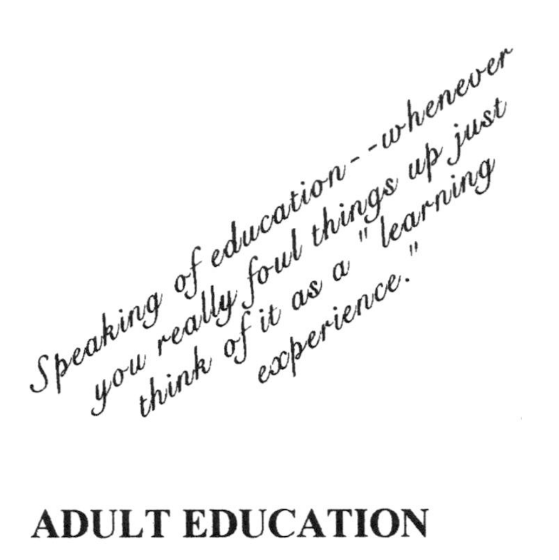

ADULT EDUCATION

I'm enrolling in all kinds of classes this year,
Putting food in my brain, not my lips.
A new kind of diet, I thought I would try it
And broaden my mind, not my hips.

No pie on my plate, for a I have date
With Confucius and tea on a saucer,
And I shall forbear that chocolate eclair
In favor of Shakespeare and Chaucer.

I'm exchanging my calories for classes this year
On computers and business machines.
And tho' in my mind it might be you won't find it,
The difference should show in my jeans.

LH

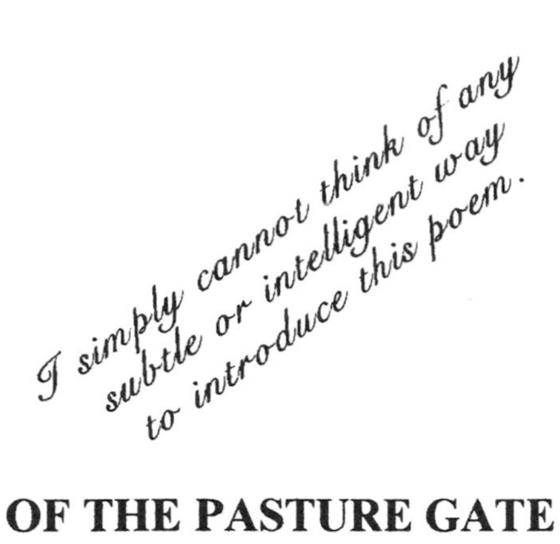

BALLAD OF THE PASTURE GATE

My husband claims that pasture fence
　　Should have both strength and symmetry,
With barbed wires stretched so tightly that
　　Maestros could play a symphony

Upon them with a fiddle bow
　　If they were ever thus inclined,
It's one of his obsessions, and
　　I must say that I don't mind

For I'm a tolerant sort of wife
　　When facing foibles of my mate.
Just wish that this fanaticism
　　Did not include the pasture gate.

Now some folks use a length of rope
　　To snub their gates and tie them shut
In varying degrees of tight,
　　Depending on their muscles, but

Ballad Of The Pasture Gate

My husband thinks a sagging gate
Would mar his fence's symmetry,
Or cause a cow to test its strength,
Or lure trespassers in, you see,

So our all have those wire loops
That hold the gate up to the post,
So snugly, with such tension, that
Only a Superman could boast

The strength to squeeze enough to gain
A little slack, and so to slide
That loop up high and free the gate
Without the loss of hand or hide.

And though I've tried most diligently,
Success for me's been minimum.
I'll pull a muscle, pop a rib,
Or catch my fingers or my thumb.

So one day when he sent me forth
To take the cows some blocks of salt,
'Twas with a faint and fluttering heart
I drew my pickup to a halt

Before that vile and vicious gate.
But, summoning all my grit and muscle,
Approached the task with derring-do,
And so began this epic tussle.

With cheek and chest against that post
I squeezed and squeezed and squeezed in vain.
And then I thought, "I'll just pretend
This burly gatepost is John Wayne."

I squeezed with vigor much renewed,
    And soon that loop began to slip
Upward. An inch. Two inches. Three.
    But then, somehow, I lost my grip,

And oh, the panic! Oh, the pain!
    For I had caught, without a doubt,
Beneath that cursed piece of wire,
    The part that holds my sweater out.

I strove to gain a little poise,
    Some dignity, some savoir faire,
But it's a hard thing to attain
    When snubbed up on short picket there.

I found I could not even turn
    And so regain my squeezing stance.
And, horrified, I realized
    To free myself, I had no chance.

My life flashed past me, reel on reel,
    I wondered which would be the worst,
To be some coyote's hors d'oeuvre,
    Or die of hunger or of thirst.

I thought about the trusty knife
    I carried in my pocket there,
Should I like Amazon of old
    Lop off my breast and bind my hair?

Or was that metaphor awry?
    I did not put it to the test.
Perhaps it was some other myth
    Who'd lopped her hair and bound her breast.

Ballad Of The Pasture Gate

The time went sifting slowly by,
I'd almost given up the fight,
When riding down that dusty trail
To rescue, came my gallant knight.

With male superiority he said,
"I've come to help. I knew I ought
To get this gate You're such a boob!"
I muttered, "That's the part that's caught!"

He finally got me loose. I wept
And checked for mammillary misfunction,
While he said all the proper words
Of sympathy with utmost unction.

But from the twinkle in his eye,
I knew that my humiliation
Would soon become a story told
In every bar across this nation.

But all clouds have their silver lining.
Through darkness shines a ray of hope.
And I have gained this small concession:
Our pasture gates now tie with rope.

Limerick which seems appropriate:

There was a young cowgirl named Ruby
Whose figure was buxom and booby.
Her horse started to buck
Now we're both out of luck
For my dignity's gone down the tube-y.

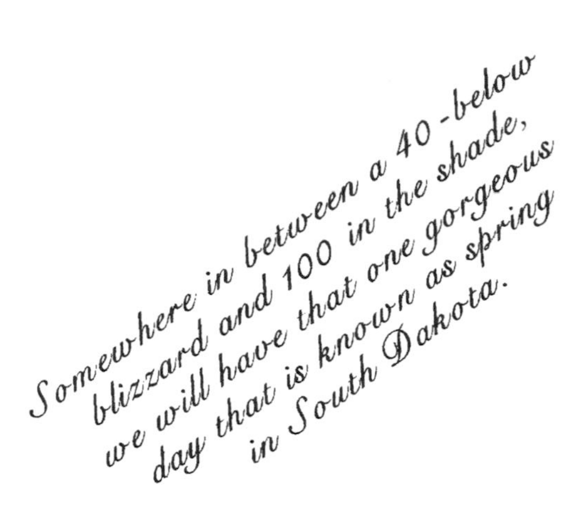

SPRING THAW

I noticed just this morning
There's a difference in the air.
Can't quite put my finger on it
But I know that it is there.

Wind is blowing, brisk, as usual,
Weatherman's predicting snow,
Yet I sense a subtle changing,
Soft, unspoken, and I know

Snowbanks soon will be retreating,
Bare spots spreading in between,
And the southern slopes will shimmer
With that first faint hint of green.

Spring Thaw

The fuzzy little crocus buds
    Will then come bursting forth,
And the wind will cease its bluster,
    Cold and constant, from the north.

The creeks will start their singing,
    Making music through the night,
And the clear blue sky will echo
    With the honk of geese in flight.

The cows are growing heavy,
    Calving soon will be begun,
But today they're standing lazy
    Soaking up the noonday sun.

Tomorrow it may snow again
    And the sun may disappear,
But I feel a thawing deep within
    And I know that spring is near.

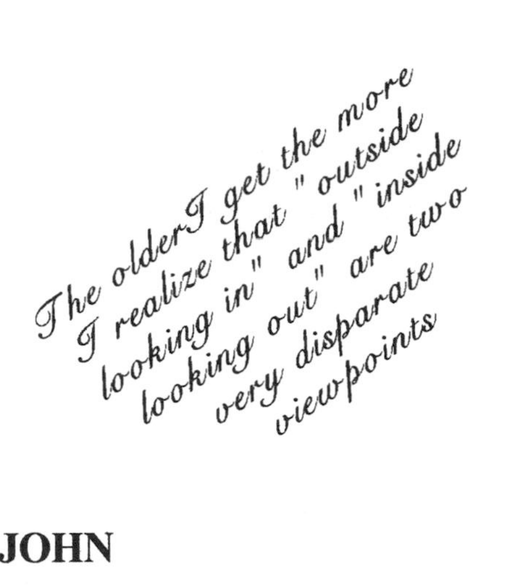

OLD JOHN

They'd always lived there in that same old place.
    They had no kids, least none I ever knew.
She was a quiet woman, strong, yet shy,
    But Old John always talked enough for two.
All bluff and bluster, so it seemed to me,
    With every word he said aimed to deride.
All through my growing years I wondered why
    She still remained there, patient at his side.

He'd take her list and drive off into town
    And leave her there alone to do the chores.
"It takes a man to get his money's worth,
    You send a woman in, she'd buy the stores
And spend the day just gossiping around,
    And prob'ly kink her hair and paint her face
And come home wearing pants as like as not.
    A woman's got to learn to keep her place."

"This pumpkin pie," he'd say, "is not too good.
I've seen fresh cowchips that have looked as
nice,
And prob'ly tasted better." All the while
She'd deftly serve him up another slice.
Then, just that sudden, Old John up and died
And left her lone. The first thought in my mind
Was "Praise the Lord! She's free at last!"
I hoped she'd quickly leave that place behind.

Be done with chores, perhaps move into town
And maybe build herself a whole new life.
Could be she'd cut her hair and put on slacks,
She'd served her sentence as a "proper" wife.
But she just stayed out there all by herself,
The mailman always brought her lists to town
And neighbors would take turns delivering things.
One night I volunteered to take stuff down.

I found her finishing the chores in John's old
coveralls.
I asked her how she'd been,
And told her if she'd like to shop herself
That next week I would gladly take her in.
"John did the buying for us both," she said.
"To pick and choose is something I can't bear.
I like the simple rhythm of the chores,
To me our way of life was more than fair.

"John always said good cooks deserved the best.
And so he'd add onto that list of mine

Such things I never would have thought to buy.
    Each time he shopped 'twas just like
                                Christmas-time."
She shook her skirt free from the coveralls.
    "I never did wear slacks like others did.
'Twas my one vanity, I guess. John always said
    That legs as nice as mine should not be hid."

She pushed the hairpins back into her hair.
    "Come in. Come in. I know I look a fright.
John never wanted me to get it cut.
    He liked to watch me brush it out at night.
I've pumpkin pie. It was John's favorite kind.
    I baked them every Friday, as a rule."
Then added softly, as an afterthought,
    "Somehow I surely miss that darned old fool!"

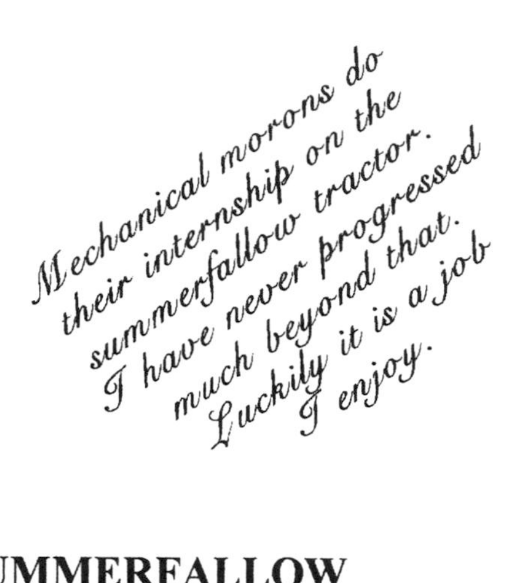

SUMMERFALLOW

Today I drive a chariot down the field
A hundred eager horse breathing fire
And I, a Phaeton, urging them on.

("Whoa, there!" I said "Whoa!")

My chariot sits axle-deep in mud.
My horses snort but only spin the wheels
And I, a wife again, go get my husband.

("Darling, I did say 'Whoa'!")

This poem is truer than either one of us cares to admit.

THE TRIP

My husband says "If you still wish
  We'll start that trip today
But if we're going to go at all
  We must leave right away."
He does not need to ask me twice,
  Into the shower I climb,
I bathe and brush and comb and dress
  In Guinness-record time.

He sits down in his easy chair
  And turns on our TV;
I pack the cooler and the bags
  As busy as can be.
Then I locate binoculars,
  The cameras and a map;
He stretches on the davenport
  And takes a little nap.

I check the windows and the stoves
  The sweat runs down my brow,
But I am packed and waiting,
  And I say, "I'm ready now!"
I sink exhausted in the van,
  Worn out with all my toil.
Says he, "I think before we go
  I'd better change the oil!"

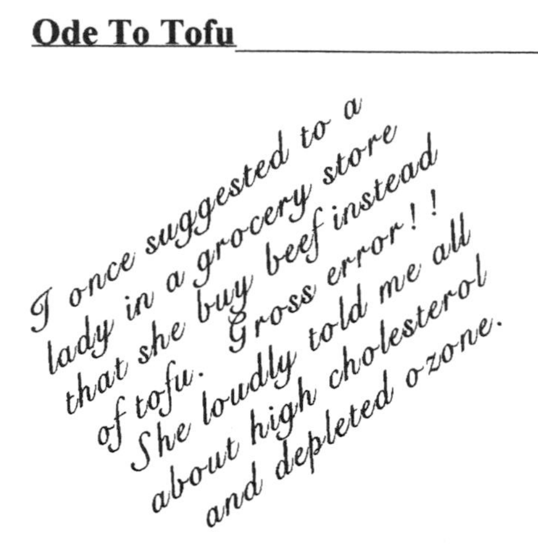

ODE TO TOFU

The gentle cows upon our plains
Who feed upon the grass,
And then, in turn, expel methane
In manner somewhat crass,
Are being blamed for making
Our atmosphere less dense.
They say someday we'll die because
Of bovine flatulence.

Does the answer lie in planting
Our range lands all to soy?
If we abstain from eating beef
Will life be filled with joy?
Let's not accept this premise
'Til we check behind the scenes,
Just how much gas will people pass
When they're only eating beans?

*If I were a musician
I could sing the title to this
poem, as it is a paraphrase of
an old sixties song.*

"WHERE HAVE ALL
THE COWBOYS GONE----"

You've heard of spotted owls
And those animals and fowls
Who are struggling with a loss of habitat.
And in all the news I read
Cowboys are a dying breed
For a reason mighty similar to that.

With the cities spreading out
There is really little doubt
That the range is getting smaller every day.
There's no room to swing a rope
Or to ride off on a lope
In the sunset. Folks are always in the way.

It's getting out of hand
This losing all their land,
The open spaces where they used to live and
thrive,
So they're heading off the range
To cultures that are strange
In a last attempt to merely stay alive.

And one has found his way
Down to San Francisco Bay
    Where he's limply putting flowers in his hair.
He's trying to fit in place
Got his long johns trimmed in lace,
    And he don't wear spurs because his feet are
        bare.

And one's succumbed to urges
To travel off to Sturgis
    And maybe join Hell's Angels if he please,
He's riding like a jockey
On a roaring Kawasaki
    With his conchoed chaps a-flappin' in the
        breeze.

And one has gotten lost in
The dear old town of Boston
    Where he's soaking up the culture that is there.
That's not coffee in his cup,
That's tea he's slurping up
    With his pinkie sticking proper in the air.

So I think I'll write my theses
On this endangered species,
    And I'll do it with all vigor and all speed.
And this will be the option:
Take a cowboy for adoption
    And you'll know you helped to save a
        dying breed.

My life is not made up of neat patterns, square corners and coordinating colors, but one can always feather-stitch over the rough seams of a crazy quilt.

THE CRAZY QUILT

This battered quilt we carry in our car
Is like a fabric mirror of our lives.

This blue's the color of the suit I wore
The day that we were married.
The skirt was narrow and was split up front
About as high as decency allowed.
He said my legs were pretty
And he grinned that crooked grin
That made my heart flop wetly in my chest
Like some fresh-caught fish pulled out upon the bank.
That was a day! Sunshine and March-green grass
All afternoon. We drove down to the Hills to rent
A rustic cabin aptly named "The Linger Inn."
That night it snowed--a full twelve inches!
We lost reverse gear trying to get out
And spent three days there waiting for repairs.
We should have known right then our life would be
No smooth paved road.
This black
Reminds me of the day my little sister died.

It streaked and ran just like my tears.
I can't believe that that was forty years ago!
I wonder what she would be now if she had lived.
At three, she read the Reader's Digest,
Perched like a chicken on the sofa arm,
Pronouncing every word phonetically.
She drew spare caricatures of animals,
Each with a fey and gentle humor of its own;
Spent endless hours with her toy telephone
Conversing with Roy Rogers.
I wonder why God took the best of us!

This brown wool patch is from a winter coat.
It's all I salvaged from the closet fire
That almost burned that poor old house as well.
(More proof that mice and matches do not mix)
Luck had it we were home and not asleep.
I thought the smoke was from my caramel rolls
Run over in the oven, 'til I saw the flames.
I sent the kids outside and got a pail
And calmly doused the blaze 'til it was out.
I had the sodden mess cleaned up when he came in,
So I made coffee, and we ate the caramel rolls.
It wasn't 'til that night I shook and cried.

I must have had some private pyromania
For he missed every fire we ever had.
The day the whirlwind caught the burning barrel
And flung the smoldering embers to the row
Of evergreens that edged the north side of our yard.
I've never seen a thing that moved as fast.

The greedy flames licked up those sturdy trunks
And hung a scarlet curtain 'cross their tops.
Ten pines do not a forest make, I know,
But I have seen my fill of forest fire.

The day the barn burned, he was plowing snow,
Breaking a trail out 'cause we needed feed.
Those were the days when we were raising hogs.
(A shameful thing no cowman tells with pride.)
But we pigged out a multitude of sows,
Fenced woven wire, and shoveled tons of feed,
--And swore a lot! But I still think we owe
Those grunting fiends a debt of gratitude.
They paid our bills while we got into cattle.

Those corduroys are from Brown Koko pants--
Those snug, suspendered shorts I used to sew
For our small son, like those the little black boy wore
In the tales we read at bedtime--interspersed, of course,
With Audel's Diesel Manual and Popular Mechanics.
He grew up quite unchanged as to his love
For books and engines and all things that turn and
move.
But not for shorts! I haven't seen his legs for years!
So in my mind, with great hilarity,
I conjure up a picture of him now--
A muscular, full-bearded, six-foot-four
--In corduroy Brown Koko pants!

Our older daughter's are the velvet scraps;
The soft, lush fabrics with their jewel tones
Of emerald and of ruby and of jade.

The Crazy Quilt

I wanted her to have the things I never had,
The clothes and parties --to lead a butterfly existence.
But Puritan Work Ethics are inborn.
She married young--a soldier; traveled far,
Packed and unpacked, made lists, cut corners,
Raised her family, and then went back to school
To graduate with honors--made us proud!

There are no patches for our youngest child.
That's not quite true--the patches on the patches there
are hers.
She trailed the others by some fifteen years.
By then the quilt had been demoted;
Relegated to a life of "take-along"
A using quilt for small emergencies:
To spread upon the ground at picnic time
Or hold, at rodeos, a tired and sleepy child,
Her red boots trailing imitation spurs
With rowels still sharp enough to tear the fabric
When she rode the buckers in her dreams.

It spent one entire winter in our living room
Draped on a table--a tepee home
For Princess One Skunk. She dwelt within,
Her blond hair hidden by black stocking braids,
Her trusty rifle ever at her side,
Sharing her raisin pemmican with good old Spot,
The best stuffed dog that ever lived.

She too is grown and gone these past ten years.
But we still take the Crazy Quilt along.
Although our children gently hint to us with gifts

Of car robes, each one folded neat in matching case,
That it, too, should be retired.
Perhaps we should perform some ritual:
A private burning as one does a tattered flag;
Or bury it with honors, an old soldier
Who has done his duty to the end--
A bugler could play Taps! Of course, we won't.
We'll keep it with us as we journey on--
Faded and frayed and frankly long past prime
--All three of us--but warm with memories.

Spring - - a glorious season!
Sometimes it reaches your heart
before it actually gets to
South Dakota

FIRST ROBIN

I saw a robin yesterday!
With feathers ruffled 'gainst the blow
He lit upon my windswept lawn,
Then tiptoed carefully through the snow.

His eye was bright. He cocked his head.
His breast was red, a ruddy hue.
He looked around in vast disgust
And then he disappeared from view.

But though the snowflakes flutter still,
I know that Spring is on her way
With greening grass and budding bough.
I saw a robin yesterday!

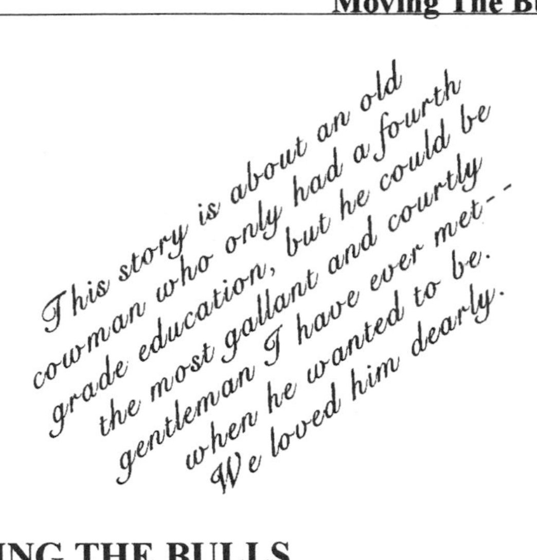

MOVING THE BULLS

Grandpa was crowding eighty,
 A really tough old soul,
And his favorite horse was Beauty,
 A mare as black as coal.
A snaky, sneaky critter,
 She was most deceitful, and
It sure made Grandpa's morning
 When she'd dump the hired hand.
For Grandpa still was young at heart
 And he liked his horses frisky,
And, in passing, I might add
 He also liked his whiskey.

He was kind of stiff and stove up though,
 So when the boys were branding
He never had a special job,
 He'd just be there a-standing,
Leaning on the old corral,
 Soaking up the sun,

Telling all those younger guys
    Just how it should be done!
But when it came to moving bulls,
    Now that's where Grandpa shown,
Though the way he went about it
    Carrie Nation wouldn't condone.

First, he'd go and catch old Beauty,
    Then he'd take a little nip
From that fortifying, satisfying
    Bottle on his hip.
Then he'd get his saddle blanket
    And he'd spread it smooth and flat,
Then take the bottle out again
    And have a drink on that.
And then he'd throw his saddle on
    As all good cowboys do,
And when the cinches all were tight,
    Gramp was, a little, too.

And, at last, he'd get a pitchfork.
    Then he'd drink a final toast
And he'd set that empty bottle
    Up there upon a post,
And he'd swing up on old Beauty
    (It was very plain, of course,
That there was this special feeling
    'Tween Grandpa and that horse.)
And they'd take off hell-for-leather
    Out across the plains,
His right hand held the pitchfork
    And his left hand held the reins.

So, of course, he'd lose his Stetson,
But Grandpa'd still be there
With the sunlight glinting brightly
On the silver of his hair.
And he'd prod 'em with that pitchfork
And he'd give a mighty shout,
And before they knew what happened
Those bulls were moving out.
Now I've been thinking, if the devil
Had been watching those bulls run
And decided that he'd come to earth
To enter in the fun,

Upon a bolt of lightning
That he'd straddle for a steed,
With shooting stars for spur rowels
Just in case he'd need more speed.
With his beady eyes a-glowing
And his pitchfork shooting flame,
Screaming like the souls in Hell,
And ask to join that game.
And if someone got a contest up
'Tween Grandpa and that scamp,
Why, I'd have won a heap of money,
'Cause I'd have bet on Gramp!

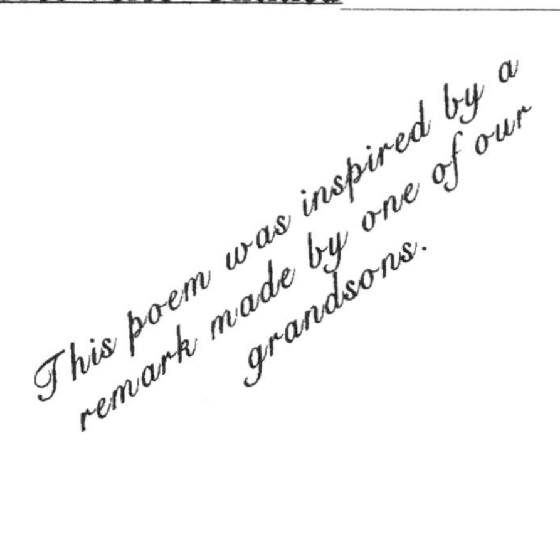

FREE VERSE--UNTITLED

Somehow I always envisioned that my life
would be different after I passed seventy.

I would sit sedately in a blue velvet chair,
Sip tea from a thin china cup,
And my grandchildren would lovingly refer to me
as "a sweet old lady."

Things haven't turned out quite that way.

I still drive my summerfallow tractor.
I have been known to imbibe a bit.
And the nearest thing to a compliment
that I have heard from my grandchildren
Is the remark that
"This grandma don't take no crap!"

Somehow, the romantic ranch life portrayed by Gene Autry and Roy Rogers is not a very accurate depiction of life here in South Dakota.

THE ROMANCE OF THE RANGE

All the glamour of the cowboy,
    And the romance of the range
That they show us in the movies,
    I consider mighty strange.
Their nights are always balmy,
    And their skies are full of stars,
And from somewhere in the background
    Comes the strumming of guitars.
Her hair is long and curly,
    And there's ruffles on her skirt,
And her boots are new and shiny
    Without a speck of dirt.
His jaw is shaved. His clothes are clean -
    (I presume so is his mind.)
And his horse is always trailing
    Just about two steps behind
He gently takes her trembling hands
    In his own so big and strong,
And at the proper moment,
    He bursts into a song.

The Romance Of The Range

Somehow while heading for our ranch,
We must have lost the trail,
For the glamour and the romance here,
By comparison, are pale.
We're out here in the cold and dark,
No moon or stars for light,
And we're bringing in a heifer
That is due to calve tonight.
My boots are pretty filthy,
And I just stepped in some more;
And my coveralls weren't purchased
At a Niemann-Marcus store.

And he's no movie cowboy.
He's looking plenty rough
With three days growth of whiskers,
And a lip packed full of snuff.
We're tired and cross and dirty,
And were chilled down to the bone.
There's no music in his cussing--
Just a steady monotone.
And 'though we're close together
And although our hands may touch
While we're sewing up that prolapse--
The magic won't be much!

So here's to cowboy glamour!
And here's to range romance!
We'd ride off in the sunset, too
--But we never get the chance!

H

Some twenty-five years ago, a man worked for us off and on for several years. He was about the best help with cattle that we ever had. And he thought that Big Timber, Montana was the most wonderful place in the world.

HE TALKED ABOUT MONTANA

He talked about Montana
    For he'd worked there in his youth,
And you somehow got the feeling
    That most of it was truth.
Talked about the things he'd done there,
    Memories from a happier past.
Talked about Montana rivers
    Running cold, and deep and fast,
About pines upon a hillside
    And mountains rising high,
About the endless reaches
    Of a blue Montana sky.

Said he left there at the war's start,
    Went to tell his folks good-bye.
Then there was a wartime wedding
    To a girl who caught his eye.

He Talked About Montana

Said she'd keep the home fires burning,
'Til the war was past and won,
Wrote her love to him in letters,
Sent him pictures of their son.
And the letters and the pictures
Helped him bear the death and blood.
And he'd dream about Montana
As he slogged through foreign mud.

They would buy a little ranch there,
And he'd teach the boy to ride.
It would be a bit of heaven,
With his family at his side.
But he came home to discover
Someone else was in his place.
She had found another lover.
It was more than he could face
For he was tired of fighting,
So he merely let them go.
It was then he started drinking,
Just to ease the pain, you know.

He'd work a month cold sober,
And then he'd draw his pay,
He was headed for Montana;
But the booze got in his way,
And he never made it out of town,
'Fore the money all was spent
And he was busted flat again,
And he didn't know where it went.

So he'd come back asking for his job,
And he'd hope you'd understand.
And you always hired him on again
For he was a darned good hand.

And he'd talk about Montana.
And you'd get a glimmer then,
Of the cowboy that he used to be,
And the man he might have been
Before war and wife and whiskey
Had bent him out of shape.
Now the war and wife were history
And the whiskey was escape.
But he swore that he was going back
And he'd do most anything
For Montana sure was pretty.
When it greened up in the spring.

Then he finally got an offer
To tend a band of sheep.
It was just for winter wages,
Barely paid his board and keep.
But it was in Montana,
So he was on his way,
He could stand to winter woollies,
He would work for little pay,
For he'd be there in the springtime
When the sky turned clear and blue,
And he'd go back punching cattle
When his winter job was through.

He Talked About Montana

Don't know why he left the sheep camp,
Started walking into town,
Maybe he just needed whiskey
To wash the lonely down.
Quick come Montana's blizzards.
Deep falls Montana's snow.
And unforgiving are the winds
When they once begin to blow.
He'd come looking for his Paradise,
He hadn't come to die.
But he froze upon a lonely road
'Neath a cold Montana sky.

My two favorite things are butterflies and windmills!

MAKE ME A WINDMILL

When I am dead
and hesitantly knock
At Heaven's door
to find no room reserved,
Don't send me back
to cower beneath the earth
I beg you, Lord,
Make me a windmill!

Then I shall see the seasons
change and pass,
Shall hear the thirsty
coming down to drink,
Shall feel your hand
in every wind that blows.
O truly, Lord,
can Heaven be more than this?

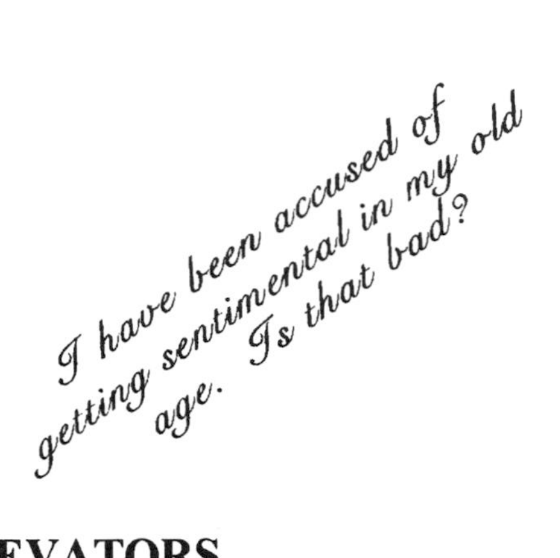

ELEVATORS

I harbor a fondness for elevators!

And when this body of sixty-odd years
Is transported from first floor to seventh
Quite effortlessly,
(Leaving my stomach somewhere between third
floor and fourth)

Or, when my husband of forty-odd years
Kisses me between first floor and seventh
Quite romantically
(Sending my heart somewhere between top
floor and heaven)

Then I feel compelled to exclaim

YEA, ELEVATORS!

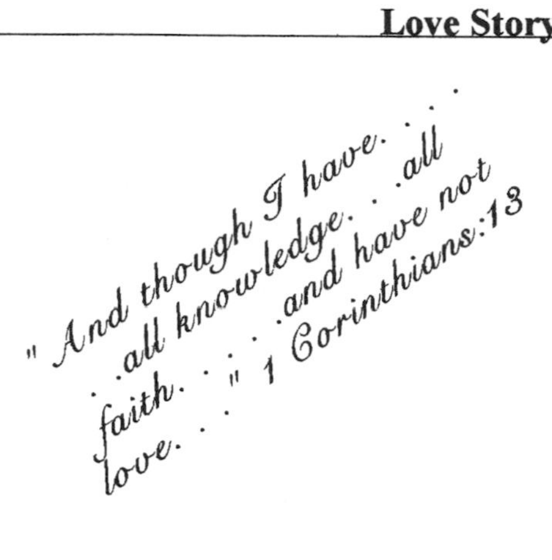

LOVE STORY

Her eyes were blue, a deeper blue
Than sunswept seas or summer skies.
He offered her the small bouquet
And told her she had bluebell eyes.

His pony's reins within his hand,
He shyly stood beside her door.
She smiled at him in sweet surprise,
No one had told her that before.

Like flowers in the springtime grass
A true love blossomed and it grew.
And when they married in the fall
The dress she wore was bluebell blue.

A little ranch, a cabin home,
Where work and children filled the hours,
And still he always brought to her
Those sweet bouquets of prairie flowers.

Love Story

Good times and hard times came and went
        But true love came and true love stayed.
But even love can't hold back time
        And even bluebell eyes will fade.

And when it came that she must don
        A widow's weeds of somber hue.
She always wore a talisman,
        A lover's knot of bluebell blue.

Oh, Grandma, with the bluebell eyes,
        What words are left for us to say?
You lie beside him once again.
        And we brought bluebells there today

I'm glad I live in a country where the seasons change.

A GOURMET'S SEASONS

The brown earth's peeking through the snow
That's melting in the sun's warm rays.
I call these early days of spring
"Whipped cream on chocolate pudding" days.

And then the earth begins to sprout
New leaves and grasses everywhere,
It's one big salad bowl of greens.
With sharp wine dressing in the air.

In summertime, when fields of hay
Are mowed and built in careful stacks,
I think of loaves of fresh-baked bread
That cool upon my kitchen racks.

And on a frosty morn in fall,
The world's one big banana pie
Piled high with fluffy white meringue
That covers all except the sky.

Then come the long vanilla months
Of snow on snow without a stopping.
How could I bear that ice-cream world
Had I not books and friends for topping?

THE CAR

My husband bought a car for me today.
A car for me to drive whene'er I choose
Without first finding out if someone needs it more.
It is not a NEW car.
The paint has lost its pristine showroom shine,
The engine is, in salesman's parlance,
Well broke in. It has some dents.
No, it is definitely not a NEW car!

But, as my husband so logically points out
---Neither am I a NEW wife!

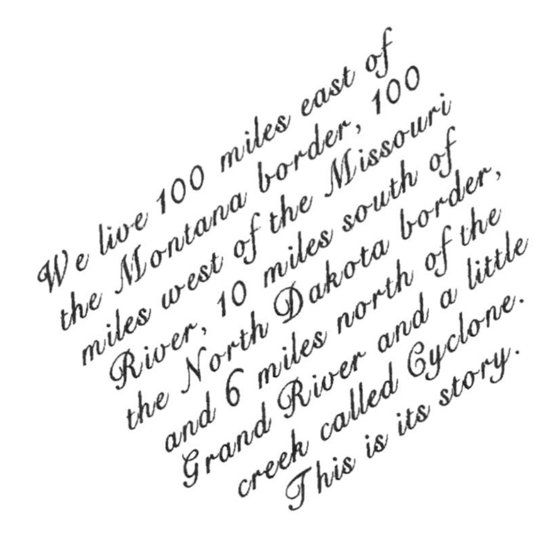

THE STORY OF CYCLONE CREEK

Cyclone Creek runs into the Grand,
And I'll tell you the tale so you'll understand
How it got its name in the long ago,
Back about nineteen-six or so.
It's not on the map for it is just
A mile-long slit in the prairie's crust,
But in the autumn the Sioux would come
To harvest its bounty of wild red plum,
And the spring-fed creek ran cold and clear
And the prairie grouse and the white-tailed deer
Could always be found on the canyon wall
Where the chokecherry trees grew thick and tall.

About a mile farther up the Grand,
At the river's bend, in a cottonwood stand,
A rancher had built a rough log shack
With a pole corral and a barn out back,
And any traveler, red or white,

Was welcome to eat and spend the night.
For the man who lived at the river's bend
Considered everyone a friend.

Now the time was somewhere in mid July
And the day was hot with a threatening sky,
The west wind blew with a fitful gust,
When riding in, all covered with dust,
Came a renegade Sioux on a jaded horse,
Running ahead of the law, of course,
Trying to keep them off his back
'Til the coming storm washed out his track.

Like a snake he slithered across the sand,
Made the sign of peace with his outstretched hand,
Held a knife in the other behind his back.
Came to the open door of the shack---
Then the lightning split the clouds asunder,
The mud buttes echoed the rolling thunder,
And the knife plunged home with a sodden thud,
And the sand was red with the white man's blood
As he died on his doorstep there, alone.
The renegade caught up a raw-boned roan,
And cold as ice the west wind blew
As he mounted that horse and led out two.
Then eerily after him down the track
Came a whirling, swirling cloud of black.
He dug in his heels and he clutched the mane,
But the thing behind him seemed to gain
No matter how fast his horses flew.
Then he came to the bank where the plum trees grew

And he let the two led ponies go
And he turned his mount to the creek below
Hoping that down there he could find
Some hiding place from that thing behind.
But the funnel followed him down the draw
And sucked him up in its hungry maw.

Next day the posse found him there
Hung in a tree by his long black hair,
With his body swinging in empty space
And a mask of terror upon his face.
The white men wouldn't cut him down,
And the red men feared that evil ground,
So they blocked the trail up along the rim
And left the canyon all to him.
And the scavenger crows picked out his eyes,
And the tree was loud with the buzz of flies;
And the sun and the wind and the changing weather
Wore away at the buckskin leather
'Til his bones dropped down upon the ground
For the coyote pups to drag around;
And soon there was no reminder there
But an old dead tree and some long black hair.

Now modern folk don't worry much
About evil spirits and ghosts and such,
It's only foolish talk they say.
But still, unto this very day,
Neither Indian nor white
Will walk up Cyclone Creek at night.

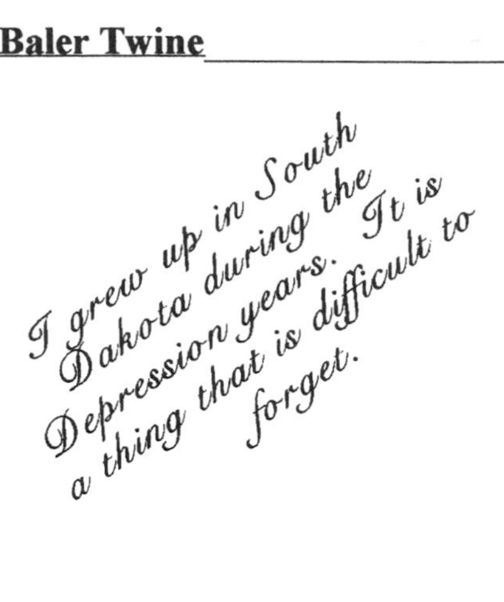

BALER TWINE

Grandma saved string. There was no piece too
short
To knot together, and add to the ball
She misered in the lowest cupboard drawer.
It makes me smile a bit as I recall
For I save baler twine. There at the start
I only rolled it up to keep things neat;
So it would not ensnare some hapless calf,
Or tangle up a loping horse's feet.

But I could never bear to burn the stuff;
I hoarded it against some unknown need.
I did not realize how deep ingrained
That long-gone grandma's "waste not-want not"
creed.
But soon each tractor and each pickup truck,
And every building on our ranch possessed
Its own and personal of ball of baler twine;
And still I salvaged, hopelessly obsessed.

I've searched for ways to use it, to excuse
This aberration from a normal state.
I've taught kids how to braid and macramé,
Made lengths of rope to hold a pasture gate.
I've tied barb wire to line posts in a pinch,
A practice never taught in fencing schools.
My husband called it "Polish fencing" but
It held the cows 'til we got back with tools.

I've brought home things like sickles, pipe and
boards,
With twine to tie them there along the truck.
Made temporary shoestrings, and I've held
A coat together when the zipper stuck.
I've staked tomatoes, made bridles for stick horses,
And even built a hasty hackamore
For a real horse; tarp straps and bails for buckets;
Tied down a hundred things, and tied up more!

My husband says he never worries much
About me, he knows I will be fine,
Though worlds may crumble and my heart may
break,
I'll patch them up---for I have baler twine.

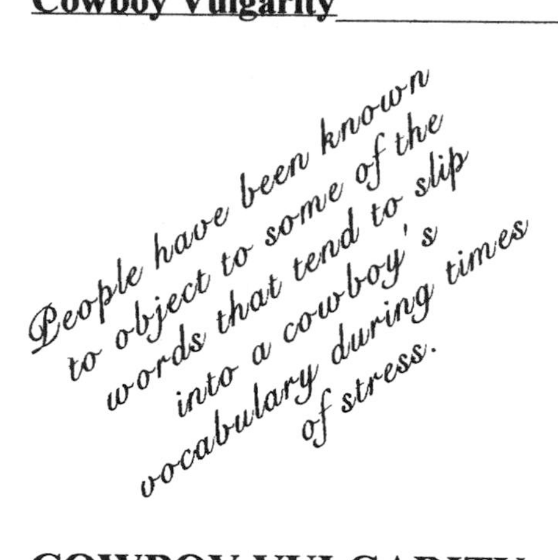

COWBOY VULGARITY

We're having problems over words
    (Folks have complained, you know.)
What should we call the stuff that comes
    From the place where cowtails grow?

If a cowboy slipped in the corral
    And on his face he went,
I doubt he would exclaim, "Alas!
    It's bovine excrement!"

Or, if he were a-preggin' cows,
    Would remark with some elation,
"I do believe I'm shoulder deep
    In fecal evacuation!"

I think he'd use that vulgar word
    That's banned by "House and Garden."
He'd say it loud! He'd say it clear!
    And then he'd beg your pardon!

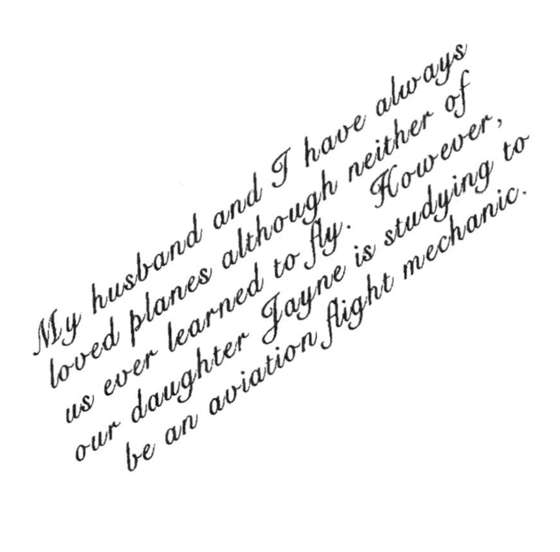

GRANDPA'S PLANE

He rode beside his father
From the time he was knee high.
He loved the land and cattle
But he also loved the sky.
Loved the creak of saddle leather,
Loved the feel of bridle reins,
By day he was a ranch kid,
But at night he dreamed of planes.

One summer day his father
Went to an auction sale,
He tagged along as kids will do
And so begins my tale.
For out beyond the barnyard,
Lying derelict and smashed,
He found the broken wreckage
Of an airplane that had crashed.

Grandpa's Plane

It had no wings or motor,
Just a battered fuselage,
But he bought it for a pittance,
Took it home to the garage,
And he washed and scrubbed and polished
'Til the old paint fairly shone,
Working on it in the evenings
After supper, all alone.

And he'd sit there in that cockpit
And dream some day he'd fly.
And he prob'ly would have done it,
But his Daddy had to die.
Just a bull that turned plumb ugly,
And a rope that didn't hold.
And the last thing he requested
Was the ranch should not be sold.

So he gave his Dad his promise
For he was the only son,
And he grew to manhood overnight.
He had a ranch to run.
He put his boyhood dreams away,
For it didn't make much sense
To be thinking of an airplane
When you should be fixing fence,

Or feeding bulls, or checking cows,
Or putting up the hay.
And soon it hardly crossed his mind.
'Twas easier that way.

He concentrated on the ranch
And all the folks allowed
That the way he ran that outfit
Would have made his daddy proud.

He loved a rancher's daughter
And she said she'd be his wife,
So they settled on the homestead
And began to build a life.
One day they wandered down into
That dusty old garage,
Found the remnants of that airplane,
The battered fuselage.

And he told her of his boyhood dreams,
Of the kid who wished to fly,
And her eyes went sort of misty,
And he thought that she might cry.
But she reached into the cockpit
And dusted off the leather,
And climbed inside and said someday
They'd fly away together.

He told her he was happy
With their life there on the range,
For good dreams never really die,
They only grow and change.
Then war came and their oldest son
Went off to join the fight.
Enlisted in the Air Corps
'Cause he thought that it was right.

Grandpa's Plane

They'd go down to the old garage
Almost every night,
And they'd sit there in that cockpit
And they'd hold each other tight.
And recite for his protection
A litany of prayer,
For he seemed much closer to them
When they were sitting there.

God must have heard and answered
For he came home safe and sound.
He swore he'd never fly again
When once he got on ground.
He'd trade the roar of engines
For the murmur of a breeze.
No plane was built that could compare
To a horse between his knees.
He'd had enough of flying,
Of silver wings and battle.
He'd spend his life just like his dad,
Raising kids and cattle.

Soon grandkids came to fill their home,
And days when it would rain
They'd go down to the old garage
And play in Grandpa's plane.
They'd dream of places they would go
And things that they would do.
And dreams can make you stretch and grow
Even if they don't come true.

Near half a century had passed
When a newsman heard the story.
He told it to an airshow,
And they made a category
Just special for an airplane
With cracked and rusty seams,
That had no wings or motor
And only flew in dreams.

And the grandkids came and got it
When the folks were gone one day,
They placed it on a trailer
And they took the plane away.
They washed and waxed and polished
'Til the old paint seemed to glow,
Dusted off the leather seats
And put it in the show.
Surrounded it with pictures
Of Grandpa and his wife
And the kids and cows and horses
And the ranch that was his life.

Fifty years collecting dust
Out in a ranch garage,
It had no wings or motor,
Just a battered fuselage.
But the judges never questioned
But that Grandpa's plane should win
A first place purple ribbon:
Best plane for dreaming in.

This poem is neither a song nor a sonnet, but it is probably as close as I will ever get to either one.

SONG FROM THE DAY THE PUMP BROKE

We fought the water pipes all day
Or rather he did, while I held the tools,
And cooked him steak for lunch, and hoped
My presence at his side would comfort bring.
We needed water soon, the stock must drink;
But nothing seemed to work. 'Twas dusk
Before we found which parts should be replaced.
I drove the thirty miles to town
Because his eye ached and his shoulders too.

I watched him through the dusty plumber's glass,
The mud-caked jeans, unshaven face,
The squinting eye. He looked so very tired
---and OLD! My heart caught in my throat
And through the quick hot tears I saw
My life's one verity, the pivot point
On which my world revolves:
I love you, and I always will, my dear.

Our son's name is John and I guess you could call this "John's poem."

THE SAGA OF THE RANCHER'S SON

One day the stalwart young son of a rancher said:

"Dad, Since ranching's in my blood, you know,
I think that I'll try rodeo.
I'll need to buy a brand new horse,
A trailer, and some gear, of course."

But- When steers knocked him on his butt,
And raked their horns across his gut,
He found his fervor much congealed,
Went home until his wounds were healed.

And then this stalwart, young, EX-steer-wrestling son of a rancher said:

"Dad, I don't have time to cut that barley,
You see, I've bought a brand new Harley,
And I've no time to rope and dally,
I'm off to Sturgis to the rally."

But- When cold winds blew across Dakota
He found that even gloves, a coat, a
Helmet wouldn't keep off that snow,
And biking was no way to go.

So then this stalwart, young, EX-steering-wrestling, EX-bike-riding son of a rancher said:

"Dad, I'm through with biking, so take heart,
I've bought a pickup, state of art,
It's got roll-bars and chrome a-plenty,
I've clocked her at 120.

But- As Shakespeare said "Aye, there's
the rub-ble."
Pickups mean girls, and girls mean trouble.
And soon this son brought home a wife,
And for forever changed his life.

So now this stalwart, young, EX-steer-wrestling, EX-bike-riding, NEW pickup-driving, MARRIED son of a rancher said:

"Dad, Peculiar things have come to pass,
I didn't know one paid for gas,
And food and all that other junk,
And hospitals take quite a chunk.

But- Ranch kids don't cost much to raise,
And I'll have help one of these days."

Yesterday, this same still stalwart, slightly older, EX-steer-wrestling, EX-bike-riding, OLD pickup-driving, MARRIED son of a rancher, and FATHER of two boys of his own, said:

"Dad, I don't know what's with kids today,
They never want to work, just play,
And they act like I'm made of money.
I can't see why you think that's funny.
I don't know where they learned that stuff.
And Dad, did you know ranching's tough?"

This reminds me of some of the help we've had.

A WINDY TALE

He said his birthplace was the plains
But he never knew his mother,
For an old she-wolf had raised him
With the wind his only brother.

The story of the mothering wolf
Seemed a little out of sight,
But we thought his kinship with the wind
Was probably half right.

For he would blow incessantly
With little provocation,
And his inflated stories were
Of interminable duration.

The words spewed forth like tumbleweeds
That roll before a gale.
Compared to his, Old Pecos Bill's
And Bunyan's tales were pale.

He never worked. He'd talk and eat.
And then he'd talk and sleep.
And so we got to figuring ways
For him to earn his keep.

We'd have him turn the windmills
  When summer winds didn't blow,
For we knew when he got going strong
  That water sure would flow.

Or when a winter blizzard
  Kept us from going forth,
We'd have him talk straight into it
  And blow that storm back north.

We could hire him out to sailors.
  He'd fill those sails real fine.
Or perhaps some lady'd need him
  Drying clothes upon her line.

Thinking how he'd wave Old Glory
  Darned near made us all salute.
We'd find a hundred jobs to fit
  That windy old galoot.

Then one day we found him stiff and cold,
  He'd drawn his final breath.
He sure didn't wear out working,
  Guess he talked himself to death.

And the strangest thing has happened,
  Though we don't know why or how,
But we've come to miss his stories,
  And we even miss him now.

S. J. and I celebrated our 50th anniversary this year, which should qualify me to do an Ann Lander's-type poem.

ON STAYING MARRIED

In these days when a divorce
Is a common thing of course,
        I suggest the best solution
                to keep those marriage vows
Is to buy a chunk of land
And, as wife and only hand,
        Go in debt a whole lot more
                and buy some cows.

I don't say that you won't fight
Over who is wrong and who is right,
        And at times you both could walk
                right out the door.
But with all that work, by heck,
And the banker on your neck,
        You will find you'll need each other
                more and more.

Say the baby gets a hiccup,
So you jump in the best pickup,
You are heading for the doctor,
don't you know.
Or perhaps some kid is bleeding,
That's the reason why you're speeding,
And you somehow hit the mailbox
as you go.

When he sees that dented door
That wasn't there before,
Hasty words will escalate
into a major fight.
He'd leave the kids and you
With no backward glance, that's true,
But he just can't leave that heifer
that is due to calve tonight.

Or you ask for help one day,
And again you hear him say
Either cows, or fence or haying
needs him worst;
Or perhaps some calves need pilling.
Well, you're tired of second billing
And you're gonna go someplace
where you'll be first.

You are through with all this grieving.
You'll just pack and then you're leaving.
It's a step that you consider
overdue.
Then recall, much to your sorrow,

That they're branding calves tomorrow,
And you guess you'd better stay
and feed the crew.

So you take it on the chin,
Muster up a little grin,
Turn it all into a story that will make
the neighbors laugh.
For there's a payment due
And this is your business too,
And it's going to take you both
to save that calf.

Now the moral to my story:
Ranching is no way to glory.
It's a headache and a heartache
and full of woe, that's true.
But when facing drouth or blizzard,
Scared clean down into your gizzard,
You'll remember two, together,
will somehow make it through.

So if you want to build a life,
Stay forever man and wife,
Buy a ranch and get a mortgage
that you have to pay and pay.
Now as my tale discloses
It will be no bed of roses,
But you'll still be hangin' in there
on your Golden Wedding Day.

Thunder Hawk, so I have heard, had more bootleggers per capita than any place in the country. This is a story my father used to tell.

OLD JAKE

Old Jake lived in a little shack
Way back behind a hill,
And he made bootleg whiskey
In a battered copper still.

Now Old Jake was a fat man
With a belly like a keg,
And he used a cane to get around
For he had a gimpy leg.

A cranky, foul-mouthed bachelor
With the manners of a hog,
Old Jake had never had a friend
Unless you'd count his dog.

That old white cur had mangy hair
You couldn't comb with a rake.
A fat, mean dog who limped and was
A replica of Jake.

But though he never had a friend,
Folks flocked to Old Jake's door
To buy his wares in pints and quarts,
And then come back for more,

For Jake made sippin' whiskey
In that battered copper still
The likes you've never tasted,
And prob'ly never will.

And some folks said that old white dog
Knew how to make it too,
For he'd follow Jake upon his rounds
Just checkin' on that brew.

'Til one day Jake called Whitey,
He called but no one came.
And though Jake hobbled 'round for days
Just cryin' Whitey's name

He never found a trace of him.
Old Jake was mad as sin;
He vowed he'd get those fellows
Who had done old Whitey in.

For when time came for cookin' off
Jake knew it would be hard
To have to do it by himself
With no Whitey there on guard.

But he went to workin' at the chore
And he found, when almost through,

A lump of something laying there
In that barrel, and Old Jake knew

That sodden, yeasty mass of hair
Was his dog, without a doubt;
So Jake reached down into the barrel
And he pulled Old Whitey out.

He must have gone to check the mash
When Jake was not around,
And somehow lost his balance
And tumbled in and drowned.

The whiskey fumes and sadness
Filled Old Jake's eyes with tears,
For he and Whitey had been friends
For near eleven years.

And Jake dug a grave for Whitey
As any old friend would,
Then he bottled up the whiskey
And declared it "doggone" good.

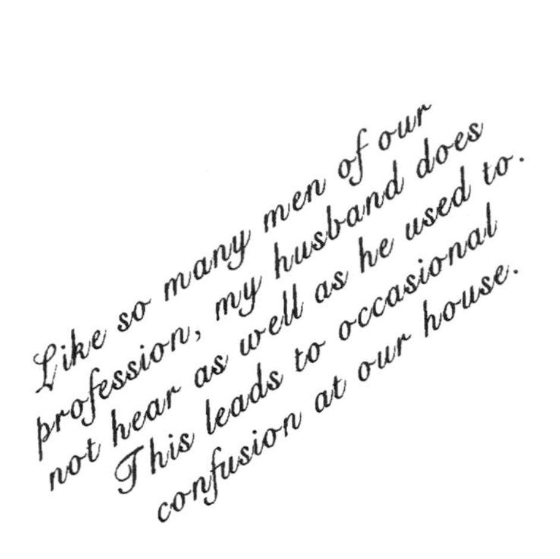

THE CEMETERY

We have a small town cemetery
On a little hill out on the prairie
And all our folks are buried there.
But there's no such thing as perpetual care,
And so we go there every spring
To mow and rake and do the things
That someone always has to do,
And all our neighbors work there too.

Last spring the graves were a disgrace
For cactus had overrun the place
And was choking out the prairie grasses
In ugly, prickly, spiny masses.
So a group of us decided that we
Would all get together one day and see
If with spades and shovels and muscles stout
We could dig those pesky critters out.

When I told my husband of our plan
(Now remember, he's kind of deaf) and Man!
He jumped from his chair and he stomped around,
And he ranted and raved, 'til I finally found
What his temper tantrum was all about---
He thought we were digging the CATHOLICS out!

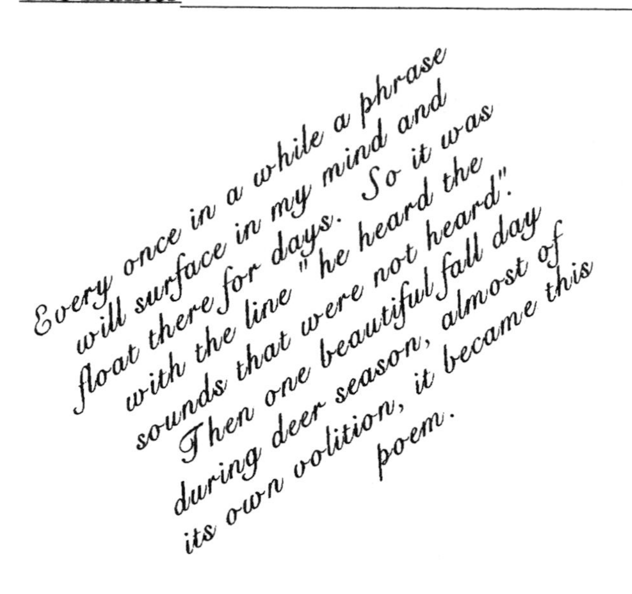

THE HUNTER

"I'll brush this draw alone," said he.
Not his the camaraderie
Of hunting friends with jovial talk.
He loved a solitary walk.
He reveled in the autumn days,
The shimmer of a far-off haze.
So down the crumbling bank he slid
Into a canyon that was hid
To all but one free-flying hawk.
And slowly he began to walk
The narrow path that bowed and bent
'Round rocky outcrops as it went
Past scarlet sumac, bright and bold,
'Neath aspens quivering with gold.
The air with sage was sharp and sweet,
He trod the trail on silent feet

Into a mystic, magic place.
The sun shone warm upon his face,
And yet there was a hint of cool.
No ripples marred the little pool,
And yet the vagrant breezes made
A dappling of sun and shade.

Forgetful of his questing, he
Leaned quietly against a tree.
He heard the sounds that were not heard,
The sudden stillness of a bird,
The sighing of a falling leaf,
And, in that world of half-belief,
He slowly turned and there he saw
A regal buck come down the draw,
Crowned like a king, for on its head
A trophy rack of antlers spread.
The man could only stare and stand
The gun forgotten in his hand.

The buck walked down the path with pride.
It did not flee nor try to hide,
But straight along without a turn
It moved in casual unconcern.
So closely did it pass him by
He saw the glisten of its eye,
He saw it breathe, the nostrils flare,
The gentle ripple of its hair.
It stepped across the narrow brook
Without a single backward look,
Its passage momentarily mirrored,
Then, like a wraith, it disappeared.

The Hunter

Was it mirage? Or did he dream?
One or the other it would seem,
Except upon the gladey dusk
The faint, elusive scent of musk;
And, if he needed further proof,
The clean, clear prints of cloven hoof
Shown sharp upon the pathway sod.
--But there was one thing that was odd.
For back as far as he could scan
He found no prints of him, the man.

The hunter pondered 'til the damp
Of evening sent him back to camp.
They hailed him, asked him of his luck.
He only said, "I saw a buck."
And slowly cased his gun, and then
He never hunted deer again.

That first year was really hard.

RETIREMENT

The cattle should be brought home soon
    But though it's now November,
We must forget---it's not our place
    In these days to remember.
For we have passed the ranch on down
    And it is better so,
For old folks have to fade and die
    And young folks have to grow.

There's grandsons riding with their dad
    As he once rode with us,
So we don't have to check those cows,
    And we don't have to fuss
And watch the weather for the day
    When autumn turns to cold,
And we can hug our cozy fire
    For we are growing old.

And we can travel far and wide
    Without a rhyme or reason,
Our life is not dependent now
    On livestock and the season.
But when you've lived through drouth and storm,
    Through hard times and through debt,
It's in your bones and in your blood,
    And it's so hard to forget.

Retirement

Now we can sleep the whole night through
When it is calving weather,
Forget the times we worked 'til dawn
To save those calves together.
And we don't have to slog through mud
To mend a broken wire;
Or watch to see that lightning bolts
Don't start a prairie fire.

We know that far north patch of hay
Is due for cutting soon,
If we each took an outfit out
We'd have it done by noon
Tomorrow, if we didn't break down
And we kept working steady,
But it is not our place these days
To say when hay is ready.

We won't go to the auction barn
Or even watch the price,
Though we went there each week for years
And visiting friends was nice.
And we won't go to bull sales,
Judge weaning weights and such,
It's not that we no longer care---
It's that we care so much.

They say remembering gets hard
When you get older, yet
I think the hardest thing of all
Is trying to forget.

VETERINARIAN'S ASSISTANT

My husband called to me one day,
He said, "Come out here right away.
I need some help to calve a heifer."
I wish I'd been a little deafer;
I wouldn't have heard that siren call;
I wouldn't have gone outside at all.
But I put on my boots and coat,
And like some sacrificial goat,
I followed him down to the end
To where the close-up cows were penned.
I spot that critter. There's no doubt,
For two small feet were hanging out.

My husband went off in pursuit.
I got positioned by the chute.
And when that cow came waltzing by
I sort of looked her in the eye

And realized we share a name,
For "cow" and "coward" start the same.
I slammed the gate with quite a din.
The cow's still out--but I'm locked in!.
Somehow my husband didn't agree,
He wants that cow instead of me.
He said, "I'll man the gate today
And you just ease her up this way."

And so I chased her 'round and 'round,
But somehow she just never found
The place she was supposed to go;
And when we'd made ten laps or so
I realized --She's chasing Me!
That's not the way it's s'posed to be!
By now this cow was plumb irate.
I started looking for a gate.
And so we made another lap,
But when I couldn't find a gap
I jumped into the water tank.
She took out sixteen feet of plank
When I sidestepped to let her pass,
And headed out for greener grass.

But when she made that final jump
That calf just popped out with a thump
And landed there upon its head,
I thought for sure that it was dead,
But then it gave a little bleat
And started struggling to its feet.
We had it dried off with a sack
Before that cranky cow came back.

Veterinarian's Assistant

My husband he is bragging yet!
He thinks he is one super vet!
He says you don't need a Cesarean
To birth the calves your cows are carryin'.
This calvin'-out's an easy life
'Cause all you need is just a wife.
You let her chase that cow around
Across the corral's muddy ground.
The cow, in turn, will then chase her
Through slush and slop and fresh manure,
And first thing that you know you've found
That calf is out there on the ground.

I don't endorse his doctoring ways
So I'm some chary with my praise.
And if he aims to be persistent
He'd better find a new assistant.

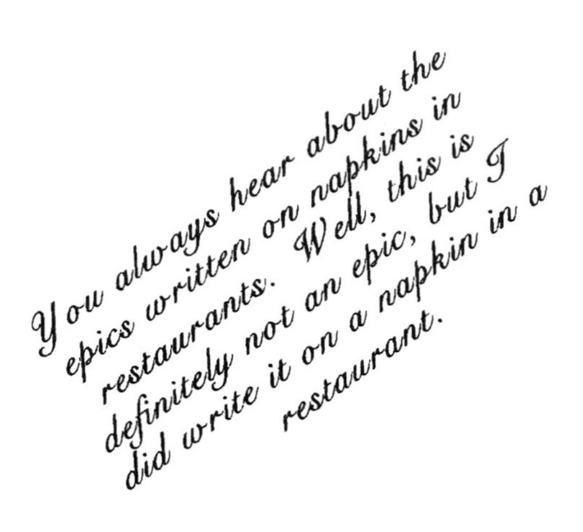

SOUP'S ON

The modern waitress of today
Wears uniforms décolleté.
I often wonder: should she stoop,
Would she fall out into my soup?
And while some folk might think them tony
Commingling with their minestrone,
Or dangling gaily in between
The lush legumes of ham-and-bean,
I'd find most gauche and out of place,
Boobs bobbing in my bouillabaisse.

If any folks ever needed to believe in Santa Claus, I think it would be cowboys

SANTA CLAUS AND THE COWBOY

A cowboy wrote a letter,
Faxed it off to Santa Claus,
And the list of things he asked for
Made dear old Santa pause.

He'd like a new Ford pickup,
A 4 x 4 with class
And lots of chrome and leather
And a Visa card for gas.

A matching trailer would be nice,
A rope that never misses,
A Stetson full of Xes
As love letters are of kisses.

A leather vest, some silver spurs,
A saddle for his horse,
A flashy turquoise buckle,
And some brand new boots, of course.

So dear old Santa went to work
To fill this cowboy's stocking.
The elves were busy day and night,
The overtime was shocking.

But every gift was finished
By sundown Christmas Eve,
The reindeer were all harnessed,
And it was time to leave,

When Santa eyed that ancient sleigh
And muttered to an elf,
"I'm tired of going second class.
I'll try his rig myself.

"It's better far than what I have,
It's time I acted smart,
But if I'm going to drive that Ford,
I'll have to dress the part."

He pulled a pair of Levis on,
Put on that turquoise buckle,
The boots with jingly silver spurs.
The elves all heard him chuckle.

He threw away his stocking cap,
Put the Stetson on his head,
Forgot about his "Ho! Ho! Ho! 's"
And "Yippee!" 's what he said.

He kissed the startled Mrs. Claus
And as the elves jumped clear,
He revved that engine up full speed
And dropped it into gear.

Folks swear that night they never heard
A single reindeer's hoof,
Just someone peeling rubber
As he took off from the roof.

When they looked out of their windows
They saw tire tracks in the frost,
Heard an engine roaring up above
And smelled the hot exhaust.

And wives complained next morning,
On the carpet they could see
Where someone with his spurs on
Had been walking 'round the tree.

Santa never left that cowboy's gifts,
Just roared past in the truck
And honked the horn and hollered,
"Merry Christmas! Let 'er buck!"

We have lost far too many of our old-time cowboys in these past few years...too many stories.. too much history.

REQUIEM FOR AN OLD COWBOY

He told us that he'd soon be moving on,
Up to a range that none of us had seen,
Where skies were blue and cloudless, and the grass
Was stirrup deep and always lush and green.

Unfenced, he said, as far as eye could see,
With brushy draws to harbor quail and deer,
Tall trees to rest beneath at noon,
And creeks that ran forever cold and clear.

The Boss the best that you would ever find,
So true and honest, One who'd understand
About cattle and the men who cared for them,
And proud he'd be when riding for that brand.

And now he's gone ahead to point the trail,
We'll stay a bit and finish up our cup,
Then douse the fire and follow where he's led.
Ride slow, old friend, we'll soon be catching up.

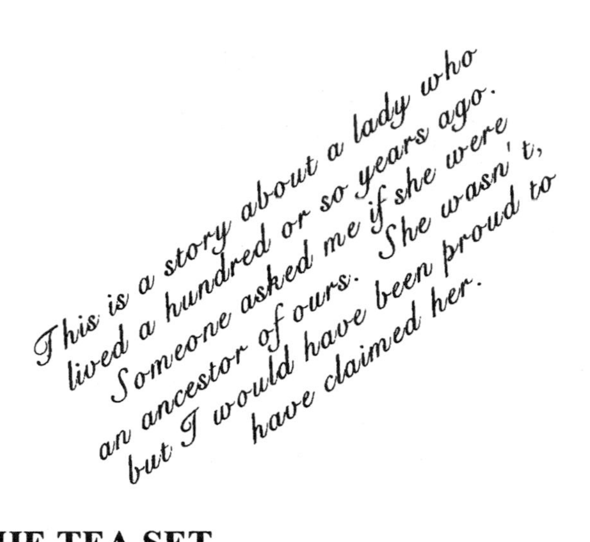

THE TEA SET

She never did quite understand
Just how she chanced to meet
The darkly handsome stranger
Who swept her off her feet.

He'd come from somewhere farther west
Said he had a ranch out there.
She never asked about his past.
Somehow she didn't care.

She ignored the warnings of her friends
And before the week was through,
She rode away, the brand-new bride
Of a man she scarcely knew.

She only took one thing with her
But that one thing meant a lot.

The Tea Set

'Twas a fragile china tea set
With a painted Chinese pot.

He sneered when she unwrapped it
And he scorned the tea she made,
And his dark and surly silence
Made her suddenly afraid.

He'd ride off almost every night
And as her tears would start
She'd warm her hands upon the pot,
But nothing warmed her heart.

She was glad about the baby,
Thought perhaps that he might change,
That they'd become a family,
Make friends there on the range.

But it didn't make the difference
That she hoped that it might do,
He only grew more secretive
And the child was sullen too.

He'd leave the ranch to run itself
And ride off down the trail,
He always wore his pistols,
And she knew he'd been in jail.

She'd be left alone with just the boy
Sometimes for days on end.
She hardly ever saw a soul.
She never had a friend.

And if she dared to question him
He'd answer angrily.
And once when he had found her
Seeking solace from her tea,

He grabbed the fragile china cup
And smashed it on the floor,
Then he slapped her and he cursed her
And he strode out through the door.

As she picked the shattered fragments up
Her face tear-stained and pale,
She heard the hooves go galloping
Back down that hell-bent trail.

They brought him home across his horse
One day at dawn's first light,
Some men she did not recognize,
They said there'd been a fight.

She asked of them no questions,
She did not want to know.
She closed the collar 'round his throat
So the rope-burns wouldn't show.

She dug a grave and buried him
Back on a little mound.
Wrote his name upon a headboard
And built a fence around.

For family ties are family ties
And each must claim his own.

The Tea Set

She only wished to shield their son
For the boy was almost grown.

But he had not died quite soon enough
For his son had learned his ways.
And he too rode the midnight trails
And squandered all his days.

They found him with some stolen steers,
He was guilty they could see.
So with vigilante justice
They hanged him from a tree.

She came and cut the body down
And placed it in the plot,
In her mind there was no question
If there was guilt or not.

She did not make excuses,
Did not condone the sin.
But family ties are family ties,
And you bury your own kin.

She could not bear to face the dawn.
She hated sunset more.
She brooded through the daytimes
And at night she walked the floor.

She railed at God. She bowed in prayer.
She struggled with her doubt.
Then, one day, she squared her shoulders
And she brought the tea set out.

She washed the thin, translucent cups
And the painted Chinese pot,
And brewed herself a cup of tea,
All clear and steaming hot.

She tallied up her losses,
Neither mother now, nor wife.
Then she pulled the ranch together
And she built herself a life.

And she became a legend
In the country 'round about.
Her door was always open
And the welcome mat was out.

She'd stir the fire and brew the tea,
All clear and steaming hot,
And fill the dainty little cups
From the painted Chinese pot.

And no one ever laughed or scoffed,
And no one called her strange.
But those grizzled old cowpunchers,
The bronc busters off the range,

And the bankers and the buyers
Of those days that used to be
Would recall with awe the lady
Who invited them to tea.

AND THEN COMES SPRING

The harvest's done. The stacks are moved in close.
  The cattle are brought home to winter ground.
And soon the snow begins to fall and weave
  A white cocoon, encircling us around.

The winds blow sharp across the frozen plain.
  The days grow shorter still. The drifts pile deep.
We settle to a set routine of chores,
  Of feed and sleep, repeated. Feed and sleep.

At last, a waking murmur in the earth.
  The sun shines warm. The creeks begin to flow.
And here and there dark patchings will appear
  Like magic, in the fast-receding snow.

The time has come for new calves to be born.
  And at this ancient ritual of spring
Our hearts will burst forth too, from winter's womb,
  And join them in their stiff-legged frolicking.

Don't try to tell me that cowboys aren't romantic!

COWBOY COURTIN' TIME

When Romeo went courtin'
He climbed a balcony,
And some men serenade you
Upon their bended knee.

Leander swam the Hellespont
To reach his lady's side,
But when a cowboy comes a-courtin'
You get a pickup ride.

Sometimes the pickup's even washed
(Will wonders never end?)
But like as not he's brought along
His trusty cowdog friend.

The dog will bark a welcome
(And you know what that means)
There'll be pawprints and dog hair
Upon your new black jeans.

The cowboy'll open up the door
And hold it while you enter.
You know he's gettin' serious
'Cause he sits you in the center.

The cowboy's reeking of cologne,
Half a bottle, you can tell,

You wish he'd shared it with his friend
    Who has that doggy smell.

A hairy face on one side
    A mustache on the other,
And both of them are squeezin' in
    'Til you think you're gonna smother.

You sit there in the middle
    Like a rabbit in a hole.
The one is merely droolin'
    While the other's droolin' Skoal.

Makes a body sometimes ponder
    On the strange queer twists of fate.
Makes you sometimes even wonder
    Which one really is your date.

The cowboy'll put his arm around
    And hug you 'til you hurt.
And then he starts to pawin'
    (The dog, that is) your shirt.

They've got you snuggled there between
    Just a pawn within their game.
It doesn't matter where you turn
    'Cause they kiss about the same

Long years have passed since courtin' time
    Changed me from Miss to Mrs.
And I'll admit, I've grown to like
    Those cowboy-cowdog kisses.

This poem is just for real cowboys!

REAL COWBOYS DO BRUSH

Have you wondered how a cowboy
Out riding on his hoss,
Far from a dentist's office,
And root canal and floss.

Eating beans and drinking coffee
'Round a campfire every night,
Can keep his smile so charming
And his teeth so pearly white?

Gunpowder is the dentifrice
Of choice, I've heard them say,
And I reckon that's why cowboys
Shoot their mouths off every day.

These last two poems span across half a century of my life. The first is one of the few poems salvaged from my teen years. The second was written some fifty years later.

WILLOWS

A west wind sways the willows
        That lean across the pond
Whispering mirthful secrets,
        And as each lacy frond
Bends to touch the surface,
        It trails the water after
In shimmering sunlit ripples
        --Echoes of their laughter.

LH

NO ONE EVER WROTE ME A LOVE POEM

No budding Keats or Shelley
Ever penned a poem for me.
No long impassioned lyrics
That scanned quite metrically.

And that is not the half of it--
No one probably ever will.
But someone picked some prairie flowers
Upon a windswept hill,

Showed me a double rainbow
And a flock of geese in flight,
Shined his flashlight on my path
When checking cows at night.

Shared smashed peanut butter sandwiches
While out there fixing fence,
Laughed at those silly private jokes
That never made much sense.

Explained the things mechanical
That I couldn't understand,
Made me believe life would be good
Just because he held my hand.

In comparison, romantic rhymes
Seems stilted and absurd,
A love poem can be lived without
A single written word.

For additional copies in hard or soft cover
or for speaking engagements; contact
Elizabeth Ebert
HCR 63 Box 125
Lemmon, SD 57638
605-374-5433